When
Elephants
Fly

One Woman's Journey
from Wall Street to Zululand

by Carol Batrus

Fulcrum Publishing
Golden, Colorado

Batrus, Carol, 1951-
    When elephants fly : one woman's journey from Wall Street to Zululand / by Carol
Batrus.
        p. cm.
    ISBN-13: 978-1-55591-565-0 (pbk.)
    ISBN-10: 1-55591-565-5 (pbk.)
    1. Batrus, Carol, 1951- 2. Americans--South Africa--Zululand--Biography. 3. Rural
development--South Africa--Zululand. 4. Zululand (South Africa)--Biography. 5.
International Wilderness Leadership Foundation--Biography. I. Title.
    CT1929.B38A3 2005
    916.8404'63--dc22

                                    2005014199

Printed in the United States of America
0 9 8 7 6 5 4 3 2 1

Editorial: Faith Marcovecchio, Katie Raymond
Cover image and design: Jack Lenzo

Fulcrum Publishing
16100 Table Mountain Parkway, Suite 300
Golden, Colorado 80403
(800) 992-2908 • (303) 277-1623
www.fulcrum-books.com

I dedicate this book to Maggie Bryant, whose vision and generosity made it possible, to P. M., whose love smoothed my rough edges, and to Jackie Batrus, who anchors my hope for the future.

Table of Contents

Chapter 1: First Glimmer

STILL JET-LAGGED, UNABLE TO SLEEP, I get out of bed before daybreak. The generator is off. I light candles; their soft glow warms the room. I pull on pants, a T-shirt, and sandals then walk out onto my front porch. Silence coats everything. The silence soothes my ragged nerves, but it allows my thoughts to take over my awareness. What have I done?

I watch as the morning sun gradually illuminates the scene. The landscape is comfortably familiar, like parts of Nevada and Utah. Open, semiarid grassland, the sloping terrain is interrupted by rocky mounds and jagged hills. This community rests on a plateau 4,500 feet in elevation, well above the densely humid tropical coastal city of Durban, four hours away. I am relieved to be here, where the drier days and cool nights remind me of Colorado, my home for the last six years. The climate of Durban would oppress me.

The sense of familiarity ends with the landscape. My brain hasn't recalibrated to the new location. Otherworldly sites and sounds penetrate my senses. The scene viewed from my front porch should be from a *National Geographic* magazine, not a place I now call home. Small, round buildings, *rondavals*, are grouped together forming homesteads, called *muzis*, that dot the landscape. The *rondavals* are built from mud bricks, or occasionally cinder block, and are roofed with thatch or corrugated tin held down by rocks. Traditionally arranged in a horseshoe shape, the *rondavals* surround a central cattle *kraal* (corral for non–South Africans). The *rondaval* at the top curve of the horseshoe houses the headman, or head of the household, the one to its right belongs to the first wife, the one on the left belongs to the second wife, and the rest house other wives, grandparents, and children. Cows and goats roam freely. It is January, summer in the Southern Hemisphere. Crops push up from a few plowed fields. A scattering of spare trees outline a creek. Grayish wisps of smoke escape through cracks in the rooftops. An unfamiliar odor, the scent of burning cow dung, disturbs the air. Very few families can afford propane for fuel, and trees for firewood are scarce.

As the morning progresses, sounds squeeze into the silence. They are living sounds, not sounds of technology or machines. I hear a man shout in Zulu. I sense he is calling to someone. Cows moo, chickens squawk, goats bleat. Schoolchildren wearing blue-and-yellow uniforms emerge from the *rondavals*, gather together, and walk along paths. Although they speak softly, their voices carry in the quiet. A truck with an engine in desperate need of an overhaul rattles as it kicks up a dirt trail while driving too quickly across the dusty, rutted road.

Avoiding the unpleasant chores that await my attention, I remain on the porch watching the community come to life. Shortly, discipline overtakes resistance and I enter my house to confront the weight of my to-do list. When I accepted this job, I knew it would be a difficult adjustment. I refused to dwell on how difficult, because it really didn't matter—I was going to do it anyway. Everything here challenges me. There are no public utilities: no electricity, phones, or running water. A small diesel generator supplies electricity. It makes a god-awful racket, so I am reluctant to turn it on during the extremes of the day. The radio-phone and the battery-powered refrigerator don't work, my water tank is almost empty, and the gas tank for my stove needs replacing. Culturally, I am worlds away and a century removed from all I have known.

The owners of a nearby tourist lodge support my presence in the community. Yesterday I borrowed a gas canister from them. I'll have to hook it up this morning. I live fifty miles from the closest town. My temporary transportation is a small car that I fear will fall apart traversing the rutted dirt roads. I'll have to wait until I retrieve my new pickup truck before I can transport the heavy tanks. The lodge has a radio-phone they graciously offer for my use. Call after call, I inquire and explain as I maneuver through systems that are foreign to me, trying to get my infra-structure repaired. A week passes. I live on tea, crackers, canned goods, raisins, and peanut butter. Eventually a serviceman arrives to fix the refrigerator. The transport fee from town is 400 rand, the cost of the repair is twenty rand and takes ten minutes. Four hundred rand is more than the monthly income of the families in this community. One more week passes. After missed visits by the telephone repairmen, failed attempts to fix the phone, and repairs that last a day, my radio-phone, one of only three in the area, works. Cebo, my neighbor, assures me in broken English augmented by hand gestures that he will have my water tank filled in two days.

Comforted by my intact infrastructure and with food in my

functioning refrigerator, I leave on a three and a half hour drive to return my borrowed car, pick up the *bakkie* purchased for my use, and bring Mac to his new home. *Bakkie* means "bucket" in Afrikaans. It is the South African expression for pickup truck. Mac is my dog. He's been staying with Danie and Linda, friends of my new employers, while I settle into my new home. When I arrive at their home, Mac boisterously expresses his good fortune that I have come to play with him. For Mac, life is one big play-date. He is ready for a road trip, but my *bakkie* isn't. The service shop has not fitted it with the safety locks and truck-bed cover I purchased. Assured that the truck will be ready in the morning, I overnight with Danie and Linda. The *bakkie* isn't ready in the morning, or the next morning, or the next. One day's wait becomes two, which becomes three, and then four. After four days in Durban, Mac and I drive my new *bakkie* home. The stage is set, the script is ready. It's time for me to star in my own personal *Three Stooges* film. I'm cast as all three stooges.

I pull the *bakkie* into the driveway and let Mac out. Nose to the ground, he races around the house gathering the smells of his new territory. I enter the house through the kitchen door. No need to gather this smell, it greets me like an unexpected fist in the face. The aroma conjures images of seriously decomposed bodies. The smell is stronger near the refrigerator. The thought of opening the refrigerator door makes me gag, but I have no choice. I go to the bedroom, find a cotton scarf, douse it with lavender and rose scent, tie it around my nose and mouth, and return to the kitchen ready for the assault. Inside the refrigerator is a revolting heap of mucilaginous rotting chicken, sour milk, and slimy vegetables. In the heat of summer, my newly repaired and well-stocked refrigerator ceased functioning. Mac enters the kitchen and quickly retreats to the bedroom. Coward! I fight off vomiting. Vomit would improve the smell, but I have enough to clean up without adding to it. I scrap the rotted food into plastic bags and place them in the trash can outside my kitchen door. I'll have to ask what I do with my trash. The smell is so awful I may have to bury it. I wipe out the refrigerator, rinse the sponges, and decide the better choice is to add them to the trash. Amazingly, I complete the task without losing my breakfast.

Time to check e-mails, my only link to the outside world; but first my laptop needs charging. I push the button on the wall in the kitchen that turns on the generator. Nothing happens. I push it again. Still nothing. I retrieve my keys and walk to the generator shed. The generator's diesel tank is empty and there is no diesel in the storage cans. I'm sure I had a spare can. No worries, I can borrow some diesel from the lodge, but I'll call first. I lift the phone handset. No dial tone, no sound at all. So much for e-mail; back to the refrigerator. I unhook the oversized truck battery that powers it. Straining under the weight, I drag it and shove it toward the truck. With one last surge of strength, I lift the battery onto the tailgate. I load an empty diesel can and climb into the cab. Mac can wait in the house.

I can't turn the *bakkie* around in my narrow driveway, so I have to back out up a hill. It started raining a while ago. The hard-packed dirt road has quickly transformed into a mud slick. The *bakkie*'s tires slip and spin. Steering is futile. The truck slides off the road into a drainage ditch. I descend from the truck to examine my predicament. The axles rest on the road, the left-side tires dangling in the air above the ditch. While I stand in the rain pondering my cursed existence, six Zulu men descend from the hills, each approaching from a different direction. Aged from forty to sixty, three of the men wear stained and torn blue coveralls, the standard uniform of laboring men, and three are dressed in tattered Western-style pants and shirts. Some are barefoot, some wear well-worn work shoes, one wears an ancient pair of running shoes. Each is clean shaven with closely shorn hair. With small nods and gentle smiles, they gesture that they will help. They wedge rocks under the tires and try to back it out. No luck. They wedge more rocks. The tires spin as the men push against the *bakkie*, rocks flying out from under the wheels. The men talk amongst themselves. Then, with a few collective grunts, the Zulus lift my truck and lay it down on the road. I thank them profusely and sheepishly drive to the lodge wondering what those men must think of this crazy white women who, hours into owning a new *bakkie*, has it stuck in a ditch!

At the lodge, a staff member tests the refrigerator battery. "Battery no good, Missus." It has broken cells and won't hold a charge. It's Saturday. On Monday, I'll drive to town to get a new battery and more groceries. I borrow diesel for the generator and drive back to my house and a dinner of peanut butter on crackers and tea. As I lift the thirty-kilogram (sixty-six-pound) diesel can out of the truck I slip, landing facedown in the mud and bruising my shin, my elbow, and my ego. Once again, I benefit from the ever-watchful eyes of the Zulus. A man appears out of the ether, lifts the diesel can as if it were a sack of air, and carries it to the generator shed. I scramble to find the right key for the shed and then struggle to open the rusted padlock. The man sets the can down, bows slightly, and departs. I try to lift the can to fill the generator tank. This morning's activities have sapped what little physical strength I have. I can't get the can off the ground. I find a small plastic pail behind the door, wipe it out with my muddy hand, place it on the floor, and tip the can toward the pail. Diesel splashes in. Using the pail to fill the generator tank, I spill a substantial portion of the diesel on my clothes and shoes.

How incompetent can I feel in one day? The day's not over yet.

I locked the padlock on the kitchen door security gate when I drove to the lodge, but left the padlock key and the keys to the front door on the kitchen table. Through the window, I see Mac racing from room to room, pawing at windows, trying to get out, clearly frantic at being abandoned in strange surroundings. I drive back to the lodge and ask a security guard for help. We return to the house and, much too easily for my comfort, he breaks the padlock with a tire iron and lets me in. I find Mac, ears down, tail between his legs, cowering behind the couch. As an outlet for his anxiety, he played field hockey with his food. Bits and pieces of it are scattered all over the house. A nice cup of relaxing tea is in order. Actually, a glass—maybe a whole bottle— of wine sounds better, but tea will have to suffice. I turn on the faucet; air sputters through the pipes. I used the last of my water cleaning up the refrigerator.

I refuse to break. Give me strength, please, God. Leaning on the sink, I breathe a cleansing sigh. A rain barrel stands outside the kitchen door. The recent rain has topped it off nicely. I fill the kettle from the barrel and place it on the stove. I turn on the stove, no gas. I look outside the kitchen window; the gas cylinder is missing—stolen. I collapse in a heap on the floor, weeping quietly. Mac comes to comfort me, licking my face and nuzzling my shoulder. I can't live like this. No phone, no electricity, no gas, no refrigerator, no running water. Rescue me, please. I need somebody, everybody, to feel sorry for me, as sorry as I feel for myself. Then truth dawns. In the States, I took these services for granted. I assumed their presence as I assume the air I breathe. No one in this place has phones, electricity, or running water. Who exactly needs to feel sorry for me? Finally, I wake up and get it: it is all a gift. My transformation has begun.

Chapter 2:
How Did I Get to Zululand?

I AM NOT A CRUSADER, activist, politician, or benefactor. I am one of the few people of the baby-boomer generation who never participated in a protest against anything, never attended a demonstration, never broke a law, and never wrote a letter to her congressman, or anyone else for that matter. Trying to balance the conflicting expectations of my parents and peers sapped my enthusiasm for cultural reform. How then did I commit to working alone in a very remote Zulu village?

As I look back over the experiences of my life, I see how seemingly small or unrelated life events all played an important role in providing the skills I applied during my time in Zululand. My path to South Africa has surface aspects—who met whom when and how—and inner aspects—how my beliefs and needs evolved so that I could choose to go. The inner journey is the more powerful of the two, the superficial more understandable, or at least easier to describe.

I was raised in suburban Washington, D.C., during the 1960s.

It was a time of revolutionary change, but not for my parents. They held firmly to their circa-1930 Middle America beliefs of right and wrong, good and bad, highly defined and separate roles for men and women. The only option I had, according to them, was going to college to get my Mrs. degree. My education was not to be used, except as an accessory to attract a suitable husband. After all, no real man would allow his wife to work, and what woman would marry a man who couldn't support her? All I had to do was learn how to care for a man, a house, and kids, then go to college and graduate with a ring on my finger.

The only time those expectations caused a problem for me was when I went to school, talked to friends, watched TV, read anything written after 1960, or spent time reflecting on what I wanted. I wanted a career, not the life designed for me by my parents. To mollify opposing needs, I made choices that straddled both paths. I excelled academically, but in the traditionally all-female field of home economics. I graduated summa cum laude with a bachelor of science degree in foods and nutrition. Seeking membership in the American Dietetic Association, I completed a required yearlong hospital-based nutritional internship at a Harvard teaching hospital in Boston. Again, I excelled academically. The internship was my first exposure to really smart people, and I was determined to prove my intellectual worth.

After my internship, I was offered a job in a place overflowing with superintellects: Massachusetts Institute of Technology. I accepted the post of research nutritionist at their highly prestigious Clinical Research Center. As my career was launched, so was my love life. I fell in love with a medical doctor conducting research to earn a Ph.D. in nutrition. The relationship did not survive. I taped over the wounds of my damaged ego, feigned indifference, but secretly longed remove myself from the scene of painful memories. My escape came in the form of graduate school, where I completed a master of science degree in clinical nutrition.

Research for my master's thesis took me back into the Harvard teaching hospital system, where I worked with pediatricians developing nutritional treatments for disease. Once I completed my master's degree I was sure I would be offered the new position of pediatric research nutritionist. Armed with diploma proving the self-worth I didn't feel, I freely disseminated my wealth of wisdom to my coworkers. Funding for the new position was delayed. I was told to take a well-deserved holiday, with the understanding that the position would be authorized upon my return.

Long story short, while I was away, the supervising doctor hired another nutritionist for the position. Graduate school was over, the summer break had begun, and I hadn't interviewed for any other positions. I was frightened and humiliated: humiliated by the sense of public failure and frightened by the time that I was going to have to spend alone while all of my friends were working. I was raised to believe that if I was alone it was because no one wanted to be with me. A pattern was beginning to emerge that I would not recognize for many years: life provides situations that "allow" me to confront me fears—a painful but highly effective learning program. When I was offered a position in a conservative community hospital in a working-class neighborhood south of Boston, I gratefully accepted. It was far below my standards of career placement, but humiliation and fear are great attitude adjusters.

On the job, my mood swung from trying to fit in and get along to trying to prove how knowledgeable I was, thereby displaying my weakly disguised sense of superiority. I was tolerated, if not warmly embraced. I made some helpful contributions, but as time passed, I felt increasingly stifled. It was 1982 and hospital cost-cutting was in vogue. Hospital support staffs' already-meager salaries were cut. With a master's degree, I was earning less than a high school dropout with a union skill. A friend who had just graduated from Harvard with an M.B.A. earned a starting salary five times mine. His advice: "Your coworkers complain that you are too assertive, fast paced, and expect too much. Put those 'awful' traits to work where they are necessary assets. You are a fool if you don't go to business school." I countered that I didn't know anything about business. He said, "What's to know? You enter business school earning nothing and you come out earning a whole lot more." It made sense. My life needed to change. I applied to business school.

I entered Columbia University School of Business in January 1983, a month before my thirty-second birthday. I felt out of place and too old to be there, but I dove in, holding on to the belief that an M.B.A. was my ticket to salvation. Naiveté had its benefits: since academic success hadn't brought me happiness, I thought money would. So I chose the quickest way to the wealth: Wall Street.

By the spring of 1984, the financial markets had taken off. Wall Street was a boys' club, and women were nowhere to be seen. I landed a position in a highly regarded and sought-after investment bank. New M.B.A. graduates were hired for a six-month training period and rotated through different departments of the firm. At the end of the six-month period, the new recruits were responsible for finding a position within the firm. If you couldn't find a placement, too bad—you were out.

I wanted a position in the equity department, preferring the diversity of the industries and the stories behind the stocks to the cold math of bonds. The equity sales manager, a known misogynist, maintained an all-male department, preferring to hire "blond boys," fair-haired young men with trust accounts. In my interview with him, he told me, "Try money markets. You won't fit in here." Money markets are the lowest rung on the institutional ladder. No way.

I asked the woman in charge of the training class for help. She commented that if I couldn't get placed where I wanted, how could I possibly think I could do the job? I commandeered an empty desk on the equity trading floor and pretended that I belonged there. Rumors circulated that federal investigators were visiting the firm asking questions about hiring practices. A few days later, the sales manager called me into his office and not so graciously informed me, "Personnel wants me to hire some women, so it's your lucky day. You have a job in sales, but I doubt you'll make it. I'll bet on it." And so my career started.

Working on the trading floor was like living in a men's locker room. The term "fuck-speak" was coined for the communication style. Stocks were nicknamed using infantile sexual innuendos. I sat and listened as my compatriots described in lurid detail the pranks and sexual conquests of the previous night. One salesman had a picture of himself grinning like a Cheshire cat with his head nested between the size–seventy-two silicone-enhanced bare breasts of a topless dancer. The senior block trader owned a battery-powered hopping penis that he would switch on and place on his desk to be chased by a pair of wind-up chatter teeth. Another trader covered the push buttons on his phone console with small rubber breasts. Lascivious comments were the order of the day.

I could have waved the flag of sexual harassment and sought legal recourse, but I would have lost my job and been blackballed. Sympathy for women earning six-digit-plus incomes was nonexistent. Most of the women in my business school class would have gladly traded places with me. The lure of big money outpaced my need for a sane work environment. The more stressed I was, the more deserving I was of the rewards. My female coworkers and I bragged about how much disrespect and rude treatment we could endure. In the mid-1980s, greed was good, stress the passport to success, and money the measure of the man or woman.

I rode the wave of financial excess, earning more money than I could have imagined possible. I played straight and ethically and did my job to the best of my ability. I calculated and recalculated how much money I needed before I could quit. My goal was never to have to work again. It was 1991. I was forty years old and vice president at a renowned investment bank, living the good life. I was in agony. My life felt shallow, without substance or purpose. I spiraled into a depression. It was my better self telling me that I had to quit.

I shared my inner struggle with a friend who had recently attended an astrology reading and suggested that I might benefit from one. What the heck—it only cost fifty bucks. I spent more than that taking a customer out for a burger. Supplied with only the date, time, and place of my birth, the astrologer told me truths about myself that I thought no one else could know. My practical self told me that there had to be a system, some way he knew these things.

I wanted to learn how the astrologer knew what he knew. He described an ancient and complex discipline in which the planets represent different archetypes, different aspects of the human experience. The planets' relationships to each other and their location in the astrology chart influence one's personality and life experiences. I bought books on astrology. I read about my planetary aspects and placements. It made sense. The books described emotions and events that were consistent with my life experiences.

Could the time and place of my birth be responsible for the challenges and gifts in my life? If this could be true, what else might be true that I had previously dismissed as bunk touted by kooks? I launched a learning crusade. I read books on dreams, past lives, alternative healing practices, and more. I met a woman who became my teacher. She introduced me to meditation, Eastern philosophy, and metaphysical thought. The depression and anxiety were lifting. I was finding answers, at least answers that worked for me.

I lived a split life, working on the trading floor during the week and spending nights and weekends studying spiritual and metaphysical disciplines. Although I didn't have as much money as I would have liked (do we ever?), I knew my life on Wall Street had to end. My emerging spiritual life was beginning to replace my obsessive need to accumulate money. The question now was, What next? Where would I go? What would I do? It was the summer of 1993. In February 1994, after I received my bonus check, I would quit. My spiritual life was putting into perspective some of my fears and my needs. But let's not get crazy—no way was I leaving before getting my bonus.

A woman I met in New York had recently moved to Boulder, Colorado. She invited me to visit her at Christmastime. In Boulder, I met a man who managed a "socially responsible" investment company and wanted me to join him. I was elated; I had found a place to go. I was spiritually enlightened and equipped with the knowledge, money, and arrogance of ten years on Wall Street. I was going west to put my money to use and save the world. Wall Street had been difficult, but what came next was devastating.

To paraphrase Maya Angelou, God always tosses you a pebble before hitting you with a brick. A brick—who cares! I worked on a trading floor, I dodged bricks for a living. I needed a missile to get my attention. The universe willingly obliged. I was conned, big time. With my sense of invincibility, I invested more than 70 percent of my savings in this new venture and it disappeared, wired to an offshore bank.

My life offered me many opportunities to adjust my attitudes, but once I decided what I wanted to believe, like a horse habituated to a trail I would not be turned. This turned me. It knocked me clear off the trail into an abyss. Did I have the courage to crawl out and face my humiliation? I could no longer cling to the belief that intelligence or money could protect me from failure and pain.

A group of loving friends emerged to support me through the agonizing process of confronting the fears and misplaced values that motivated my choices. A woman who became a dear friend gave me the courage to hold my head up and face what I had done through one comment, one act of kindness. She said that what had happened to me wasn't about how smart or well intentioned I was. It was a cosmic lesson in values, power, false gods, and real strength. My needs, combined with my fears, blocked my ability to see what was so obvious to others: the man was a con. This was an opportunity to learn what many people never learn, the truth about real power, love, and self-worth.

Dealing with my losses forced me to confront my challenges with relationships, issues of control, money, and personal boundaries. I was forced to clarify my values and defend my ethical foundations. Through reading, meditations, seminars, workshops, walks in the mountains, and conversations with friends, I focused on emotional healing. Over the next few years, I learned to forgive myself for whatever illusions I had about not being good enough. I faced the insecurities that led me down the path of self-undoing. I discarded fears. I learned the power of compassion over criticism. I accepted that all people have strengths and weakness and that the greatest act of charity is not to judge another. It was time to walk away from my losses, thank life for the lessons, and move on.

I needed a job, but what kind of job and where? I wasn't starting a new business—those scars were too fresh. Maybe a change in location would inspire me. I traveled the West, but no place beckoned. My next option was to get a job teaching and see where that took me. I updated my resume and mailed it to colleges and junior colleges. With an M.B.A. from a prestigious school, a stellar academic record, and a career at one of the finest firms on Wall Street, I was eminently qualified to teach entry-level business or finance. I wasn't looking for big bucks, just a job in a place that I liked. I sent out the resumes and waited. Nothing. No responses. *Nothing.* How was this possible? I contacted a few schools. They said I needed more academic experience. The old Carol thought, "Drop dead, you idiots." The new Carol thought, "I must not be on the right path."

After all I'd accomplished, why did I feel so stuck? Dazed and disappointed, I sat on my couch reflecting on my life. I'd built a definition of who I was and what I wanted that was so limited it enclosed me. I hid in that enclosure pretending I was safe. It didn't keep me safe; its walls just blocked my view. It was time to climb over the wall and see what was out there. A week later, a completed application to join the Peace Corps is lying on my dining room table when the phone rings. A friend with whom I have been out of touch for several months, Sally, is calling. She works as a consultant for environmental nonprofits. When I tell her I am joining the Peace Corps, she shrieks with delight. "I have something better. You are perfect." The WILD Foundation, a U.S. environmental nonprofit, is initiating a community development program in South Africa. WILD wants a person to live on-site as its manager. Sally says she will contact the people in charge of the program, but she knows that they will want me. Can I be on a plane in two weeks to meet her in South Africa to check it out? A tingling sensation moves down the arm holding the phone. I take a breath—"Yes, I will do it."

Chapter 3: Checking It Out

THE WILD FOUNDATION'S MISSION is to promote, protect, and sustain wildlands and wilderness areas across the globe. WILD's efforts have dramatically increased awareness of the social, spiritual, economic, and scientific value of wilderness. The foundation promotes species' preservation through the Cheetah Conservation Fund and elephant programs in Mozambique, Botswana, Angola, and Mali. It has nurtured many grassroots conservation organizations and collaborated with established conservation groups, influencing numerous conservation and environmental initiatives.

Although The WILD Foundation works in a variety of environmental and conservation arenas, it is best known for convening the World Wilderness Congress (WWC), the longest-running international public forum on wildland and wilderness issues. The WWC was the inspiration of WILD's founder and internationally renowned conservationist Dr. Ian Player and his friend Zulu game guide Magqubu Ntombela. The 1st Congress convened in South Africa in 1977. Dr. Player assembled an international group of environmentalists, conservationists, and policy makers in his home country to discuss issues surrounding the declaration and preservation of wilderness areas. Despite apartheid legislation banning black participation in public events, Dr. Player courageously put people of all colors together on stage.

The accomplishments of the congresses have been numerous, including increased awareness of the vital role wilderness plays in human life. Dramatic legislative advances and the declaration of large additions to wilderness areas worldwide are a result of this congress. Scheduled to meet every three to five years, the congress returns to South Africa for its seventh year, after assembling in Australia, Scotland, the United States, Norway, and India.

Mrs. Magalen (Maggie) Bryant, a noted philanthropist and environmental advocate, is a member of WILD's board of directors. In 1998, Mrs. Bryant, in partnership with Miss Mary Pat Stubbs, began construction on a cultural tourism lodge near a historic battlefield of the Anglo-Zulu War. The story of their partnership defies credulity. In 1997, Pat and Maggie, two sixty-something-year-old Americans, met for the first time on a South African Airlines flight, each returning from a visit to South Africa. Talk about fate. Initially, they sat in separate rows, but in an effort to seat a husband with his wife, Maggie and Pat moved to adjoining seats. Over martinis they discussed their mutual love of South Africa and its people. They talked about what fun it would be to build a tourism facility to promote Africa's beautiful land. By the end of the flight, seventeen and a half hours to be exact, they agreed to move ahead with the project. The Isandlwana Lodge opened in May 1999.

Boosted by the presence of the new upscale lodge, the Isandlwana area is the focus of a small but growing tourism industry. The presence of foreign tourists provides economic benefit, but also increases exposure of the economic haves to the economic have-nots, frequently a recipe for trouble. Maggie understands the potentially destructive power of foreign influence. She approached Vance Martin, WILD's president, with a request that WILD establish a community development project to help the tribal members reclaim their cultural heritage and improve economic opportunity. Maggie generously offered to underwrite the ongoing cost of the project. Although outside WILD's primary mission, the foundation's many longstanding, close, and trusted personal relationships in kwaZulu Natal support Vance's choice to undertake this project. Plus, WILD can work toward reviving the tribe's appreciation of the land and their relationship to it, both somewhat lost over years of colonial rule and Western influence. His plan is to train local people to take over the project after a two-year residency by a WILD associate. Maggie asked Sally to locate a candidate for the job.

Since I have never traveled to Africa, Maggie and Vance agree that it is important for me to visit the area, meet the people, and introduce myself to the tribal leadership before I take the job. After a fourteen and a half hour plane trip, I land in Johannesburg at 8:00 A.M. local time, disoriented and grateful to have my feet on the ground. Sally, who is working on another project in South Africa, is my in-country traveling companion. She greets me at the airport. We rent a car and buy a road map for the six-hour drive from Johannesburg to Isandlwana in the province of kwaZulu-Natal.

kwaZulu-Natal was formed through a merger of the British colony of Natal and the conquered land of kwaZulu, which was taken from the Zulus during the Anglo-Zulu War. *kwa* means "the place of" and *Zulu* means "people of the stars" or "people of the heavens." We were on a trip to the place of the stars. Hollywood? Not exactly.

Our map bears little relationship to the roads we travel. For added excitement, we have no experience driving on the left side of the road. South Africans drive faster and tailgate closer than Californians, which is to say they drive like lunatics. We want to arrive at the lodge in daylight, but with wrong turns and panic pullovers generously peppered by nervous laughter after near head-on collisions, we arrive after dark in dense fog and drizzle. Without streetlights, house lights, or moonlight, it is quite startling how dark dark can be. Thank goodness the lodge has a generator and lights, or we would not have found it until sunup.

The lodge is a uniquely beautiful glass-enclosed stone-and-thatch building. Pat Stubbs greets us and shows us to our rooms. We freshen up and return to the dining room to enjoy an expertly prepared meal. After dinner, exhausted from our highway hijinks, we retire for the evening. The next morning I begin my exploration.

The focal point of the community is a cluster of buildings with corrugated tin roofs painted a deep coral pink. It is St. Vincent's Anglican Mission, built in the 1880s after a massive British defeat at the hands of the Zulus. A simple stone church shaped like a cross anchors the complex. An old wooden bell tower fitted with a bell and a long pull cord stands in the churchyard. The church is flanked on one side by a Western-style single-level home constructed of cinder block, the minister's residence, and on the other side by the visitors center for the nearby battlefield. An Anglican convent surrounded by vegetable gardens stands across the dirt road from the minister's house. Two Western-style houses face the visitors center. Amafa, a quasi-governmental agency charged with the responsibility of preserving Zulu historical sites, built these houses. The manager of the mission complex and battlefield lives in one; the other stands empty. The plan is that if I accept the job, I will occupy the empty house.

When people refer to Isandlwana, they mean the small settlement that emerged around the historic battlefield. In 1879, the Zulus dealt the British their worst defeat in history there. The British had demanded demeaning concessions of the Zulu chief, hoping that pride would force him into battle. Armed with guns and cannon, the British believed they would make short shrift of the Zulus and claim their land as the spoils of war. History has proven that it is very dangerous to underestimate one's enemy. Several decades earlier, the Zulu king Shaka had built a military social order based on fierce discipline and training. Zulus were warriors, trained to live on little food while marching forty to sixty miles per day for up to two weeks after which they could run fourteen miles per hour when charging into battle. By comparison, the British troops, laden with heavy equipment and supplies, could move only two and a half miles per hour. On January 22, 1879, 20,000 Zulu warriors, revved up on indigenous stimulants and psychotropic plants, launched themselves into battle. The British troops were wiped out. The battle was a turning point in the history of South Africa. The British, resentful of their defeat, retaliated with overwhelming force, crushing the Zulus.

The battle of nearby Rork's Drift occurred the evening of the Battle of Isandlwana. The Zulu army, returning from their victory at Isandlwana, attacked the Rork's Drift supply depot. Fewer than 140 Brits held off the Zulus. Some historians believe that the Zulu army, exhausted after their victory at Isandlwana and impressed by the small British force's zeal in defending the supply depot, retreated with their wounded, sparing the remaining soldiers. More Victoria Cross medals were awarded for the Battle at Rork's Drift than for any other battle in British history. The 1964 film *Zulu*, which launched the career of actor Michael Cain, depicted the Battle of Rork's Drift.

The Zulu tribe residing in the area is called the Mangwe-Buthanani. Its 17,000 members inhabit 100 square kilometers of tribal land. If I had been asked upon arrival to guess how many people live on the land after only seeing the battlefield area, I would have guessed 1,000. Most of the tribal neighborhoods are hidden from view, tucked behind a rise, around the curve of a hill, or on top of a plateau. In 1999, the community has no utilities: no electricity, running water, or phones. There are few cars and even fewer roads. Much of the traditional way of life continues but is increasingly pressured by the forces of modernity.

I visit Dundee, fifty miles away, where I will conduct all of my business, banking, and weekly shopping. A town of 28,000, it was settled by coal miners. The mines are now closed, so the economy is mainly agricultural with some tourism, but the area struggles to survive in the ever-changing economic climate of rural South Africa. Dundee looks like any working-class town in an American agricultural area, but with many more black faces than white.

I meet the tribal chief and a few tribal councilmembers. The thirty-something-year-old chief speaks English and is enthusiastic about outside assistance. I visit the schools. The buildings are bare industrial block structures with concrete floors, broken windowpanes, and no playgrounds. The children sit four to a bench—on benches designed for two. The two in the middle squeeze together and the two on the outside sit sideways with just their "sits" bones resting on the bench edge. Each classroom has a blackboard and little else in the way of supplies. One child has a string tied around his neck with a pencil stub attached to the end. I ask why. It is the only pencil in his family; he can't afford to lose it. Despite the dreary surroundings, the children greet me with warm, timid smiles and bright, shining faces. They sing a song of welcome. I see hope in their eyes.

I see what I need to see. I will have a house to live in with a toilet, shower, and kitchen. The town grocery offers familiar foods, not the quality I am used to, but at least the fundamentals: milk, butter, cheese, bread, eggs, chicken, rice, beans, noodles, some fresh fruit—especially oranges and papaya—and vegetables such as cabbage, butternut squash, and chard. Although South Africa has eleven official languages, English is the main language, and the province of kwaZulu-Natal has the largest English-speaking population of all the provinces. Everyone in town speaks English. Many tribal members understand a few words of English and a few tribal members understand enough to help me translate.

For the first time in my life, I am knowingly making a decision based solely on intuition, not intellectually weighing the pros and cons. I trust my feelings. It feels wonderful. I don't need to have all the answers or to have a specific game plan spelled out. I will get things started, supply expertise, training, and anything else necessary to help the people help themselves: a perfect job for a person who needs to loosen up and let life flow. The voice in my head tells me I can do this. I accept the position as an expenses-paid volunteer for The WILD Foundation.

I return to Boulder to "de-stuff" myself, to unhook the tether to my safe existence. Over the years, I have managed to accumulate a lot of things. Shedding a home, most of its contents, and a car is a transformational process. I am surprised by which belongings are easy to part with and which are not. Furniture is easy. The dining room table that seated sixteen given to me by my mother many years ago? Don't need that. It represents a dream that isn't going to become a reality. My dressy, expensive clothes leftover from my Wall Street days are more of a challenge. They represent an image of myself—rich, seemingly successful, fit, elegant, and in charge. I thought I had disabused myself of those illusions, but apparently not completely. It takes several trips to thrift stores to clear the closets. I leave Boulder believing we all need a lot less stuff than we think.

Although a volunteer, I need a South African work visa—not easy to get. WILD, well connected in kwaZulu–Natal, is able shorten wait time. My visa is issued in December 1999. I spend Christmas with my family, who are "cautiously optimistic" about my new direction. They decided long ago that I am a little strange and resigned themselves in fretful silence to my nontraditional life choices. I decide to begin the new millennium in transit to my new life in South Africa. I leave on December 30, 1999, planning to spend one night in route visiting Mrs. Bryant and then on to Africa, in flight over the Atlantic at midnight on New Year's Eve. Apparently, South African Airlines do not share my cavalier attitude about Y2K. On December 30, they cancel the New Year's Eve flight. I spend New Year's Eve with Mrs. Bryant and her family and board my flight to South Africa on New Year's Day 2000.

Chapter 4: In the Village

I ARRIVE IN SOUTH AFRICA on January 2, 2000, excited about the adventure and slightly numb to the enormity of the change. I move into the vacant house across from the visitors center in the mission complex. The leadership from Amafa agreed that I could live in the house until WILD (meaning me) built another residence. The mission complex created "Downtown Crossing," the intersection of the two main transportation arteries—two narrow dirt roads. One road passes by the visitors center, dead-ending at the lodge, and the other road travels up the hill past my house, ending near the tribal court, the meeting site for the tribal council. I live in the thick of the action, as it were.

Pat lived in this comfortably furnished house during the lodge's construction. It is equipped with all the luxuries of home, more or less. A generator shared with the minister's house, the convent, and the site manager's house supplies electricity between 6:00 and 10:00 P.M.—that is if it is working and they have diesel. The house has a small private generator if I need electricity at other times. A truck battery, which charges when the generator is running, powers the refrigerator. A large water tank behind the house, filled when the site manager pumps water from a shared borehole (South African for water well), supplies water. The house has a solar-powered phone that sends a radio signal via transmission towers to a central receiving station. When I move in the water tank is almost empty, the borehole pump is broken, and the phone doesn't work. Actually, the pump and the phone rarely work, but I don't know that yet.

While living in this house I elevate water conservation to an art form. One morning after getting out of a bath, four inches of water to be precise, I decide to do laundry. After all, how dirty can the water be? I pour in some detergent and throw in my dirty clothes. I step into the tub and tromp around to agitate the clothes, recalling images of barefoot Italians stomping grapes. I drain the tub, stomp out the soapy water, add some fresh water for rinse, and run around some more. I pick up each piece, wring it out by hand, and set it on the toilet. When I am done, I hang the clothes on a rope in the yard and then use the rinse water to mop my floors. There are many benefits to this procedure. One, I end up with very clean feet; two, it is a great upper body work-out; and three, I learn to never take water for granted.

My first assignment is to assess the community's needs. I have no knowledge of the sociology or economics of indigenous cultures, but I won't let that stop me. I have common sense and I have people to advise me. Vance, Dr. Player, and numerous WILD associates have considerable experience plus relationships with South Africans who live and work in the province. The good news is that South Africans have knowledge; the bad news is it comes with the history and prejudices of generations of apartheid, violence, and economic dislocation.

Vance makes introductions by e-mail, Pat offers other contacts, and I begin an interviewing process. Some white South Africans suggest building an airport for easier access to the lodge. Others think a computer training facility is a good idea (probably need electricity first). Improving the educational system, supplying more water, eliminating poverty, and, of course, curing the gargantuan AIDS epidemic are other suggestions. (Maybe I could create world peace while I'm here.) I encourage the Zulus' suggestions too, but they are shy about expressing their ideas, especially to outsiders. Even with each other, they can be quite indirect. Getting their opinions will take time. I need to observe the community and form opinions of my own.

Zulus live in a very hierarchical culture. The tribal area is divided into four sections called wards; each ward has an *induna* (headman), and under each *induna* are four councilmen, each responsible for an area of the ward. The *induna* and councilmen are elected; the tribal chief, called an iNkosi (in KO see), and the royal family inherit their positions. The *indunas*, councilmen, iNkosi, and members of the iNkosi's royal family (males only) comprise the twenty-seven-member tribal council, also referred to as the tribal authority, which is the governing body in the tribal area. Everything that goes on in the tribal area must be put before the tribal council. Once a person or event is presented to the council, it is "official" and can then be recognized and dealt with by their system.

Before I can work in the tribal area, I have to be presented to the tribal council and it has to be by someone known by them. A consultant to WILD, a fluent Zulu linguist and political figure, presents me. I am asked to talk about why I am in the village, how long I plan on being here, and my intended activities. I don't want to come across as an arrogant outsider who has come to "show them the way." I want the tribe to know I respect their beliefs, traditions, and procedures. I am here to work collaboratively with them, to provide information and resources to assist them in achieving their goals. At the end of my talk I am asked only one question: How do we know you will do what you say you will do? That question provides a penetrating insight into their issues with me and other outsiders and points to how I should proceed. Gaining their trust will be my first objective. I must never make an offer, even casually, unless I absolutely know I can deliver on it. If I start by disappointing them, I will have an impossible time rebuilding WILD's credibility. I tell them that they can't know I will do what I say I will do. They will have to listen to what I say and then watch what I do. Out of this meeting comes my prime directive: underpromise and overdeliver.

After years of white rule and cultural subjugation of women, it is highly unlikely that I, a white female foreigner, will ever be fully accepted and trusted by the Zulus. Despite this, I want to make a sincere effort to participate in local activities. The church, a central force in the community, is a convenient and politically neutral starting point. St. Vincent's is one large room shaped like an elongated cross. Plaster and once bright but now faded paint covers the interior fieldstone walls. The front altar appears to be like most simple church altars, covered by a cloth with candlesticks, plastic flowers, and pictures of saints. Narrow wooden benches fill the main hall, seating about 150 people. A large concrete baptismal font, the paint faded and chipped, takes up much of the floor space in the rear of the church. From a photograph of the interior, one would never suspect it is in Africa. You would have to hear the service—then you would know.

The minister's wife, Beatrice, most often referred to by her Zulu title, Mama Umfundisi, was raised in Durban and speaks excellent English. *Fundisi* means "minister," Mama Umfundisi means the "minister's wife." Although she and her husband have only lived in the village for a few years, her role as the minister's wife puts her in a place of influence and information flow. Beatrice was of invaluable assistance to Pat when she arrived in the village. She extends a gracious welcome to me and suggests that I arrive at church about 9:30 A.M., thirty minutes after the official start, but as I soon learn, early by Zulu standards. At church, she greets me warmly and introduces me to several women from the Mothers Union; none speaks English. The Mothers Union is a church organization whose married female members help the less fortunate and oversee church activities. They wear black skirts, white blouses, and black hats.

One member hands me a Bible and a hymnal written in Zulu. I bought a primer on Zulu pronunciation. I cannot understand the language, but I can read along in a very elementary way. The Zulu language has three main click sounds, with three or more variations on each. The X sound is the sound one makes on the inside cheek when trying to get a horse to move along. The C sound is like the *tut-tut* made with the tongue behind the lower front teeth that you might give a child who is misbehaving. The Q sound is made by sucking the tongue off the roof of the mouth. It should sound like a cork popping out of a champagne bottle. Another challenging sound, the *HL* combination, resembles a very wet Bronx cheer made with the tongue inside the mouth. The goal in pronouncing it is not to spray saliva onto the person one addresses. The parishioners laugh along with me as I spittle and cluck my way through songs and prayers.

Traditional Anglican music is paired with Zulu lyrics. Zulu cosmological concepts morph into the Christian hierarchy. God—Nkulunkulu—the great one, the one of all; Jesus—the iNkosi of the *amakosi*—chief of the chiefs. The serene traditional hymns combined with the clicks and tones of Zulu feel like chocolate sauce on pickled herring—putting two things together that don't belong. After the initial shock of the Anglo-Zulu blend, I reset my expectations and listen without a preconceived notion about how church should sound. The music merges cultures, beautifully so—a metaphor and inspiration for my job here. Zulu gospel music enlivens the service. Just about the time I drift off during the sermon, the parishioners launch into a gospel and I am on my feet like a dozing desk clerk newly injected with caffeine. The churchgoers love that I try to speak the language and are impressed when I get into the rhythm of the exuberant Zulu hymns, clapping, swaying, and stomping my feet. They didn't think white people sang like that in church.

I am lucky to have my early days in the village blessed by the best of Zulu culture—the singing and dancing. With support from WILD, the tribe sponsors a contest for local singing and dancing groups to commemorate the anniversary of the famous Battle of Isandlwana. Groups from adjacent tribal areas are invited to participate. The iNkosi, with three people from the tribal council, arrive unexpectedly at my house at 7:30 A.M. on January 20, the day of celebration, to pick up supplies. I struggle to adapt to people stopping by at all hours without notice. I was raised to believe that a well-bred person never stops by unannounced, one always calls first. With no phones, that rule of etiquette goes out the window.

The festivities begin with a sermon at St. Vincent's given by a Zulu minister from St. Augustine's, an older and larger Anglican mission in an adjoining tribal area. To cater to the whites assembled for the commemoration, the sermon is given partly in Zulu and partly in English. Reverend Zulu (Zulu is a surname as well as the tribal name) speaks on what people inherit. He wisely notes that we inherit hate just as we inherit love, and it is ours to choose which path we take. As Latin incantations meld with Zulu words, Anglican robes flow beneath Zulu headdresses, and hymns are sung by people from both sides of a war, past violence and hatred transform into love, at least under the roof of this church.

The song and dance contests are scheduled to begin as soon as the church service ends. The contest area is set up in a field near the primary school. It is the peak of summer in the Southern Hemisphere. A tarp tied to poles functions as an awning to protect the honored guests from the intense sun. Fortunately, I am one of the honored guests. I sit next to iNkosi, who is dressed in Western clothes. *Amakosi* (plural for iNkosi) from the neighboring tribal areas arrive in traditional Zulu costumes: antelope skins worn as loincloths and twisted strips of leopard skins encircling their heads. Each iNkosi carries a stick or staff as a symbol of authority. The *amakosi* are an imposing bunch. Yet for all their fierce appearance, they are surprisingly jovial and love to tease. The iNkosi translates some of what they say. I suspect some is not meant for my ears. There is a lot of joking about who I am, why I am here, and why I am unmarried. An unmarried woman my age is a freak in this culture. What is wrong with me? I don't appear to be unsuitable, but who can tell what appeals to white men?

The contests, scheduled to begin at 10:00 A.M., start at 1:00 P.M. Right on time by the African clock. The first group to sing is a gospel group. Their joyful song rises out of the earth and shoots straight up to heaven, an offering in praise of God. Various groups sing traditional chants and Lady Smith Black Mambazo songs. Each group sings as a rhythmic celebration of life. The sound energizes my body and soothes my heart. I am in bliss.

Zulus are the most energetic dancers in the southern African region. Their dancing is powerful, athletic, erotic, celebratory, and threatening. The drumbeats travel along the ground, entering my body through my feet, pulsing in my chest. The performers are transformed into a blend of man, animal, and nature—connecting to the earth, connecting to the source of all life. The sounds and movements feel familiar: can humans have collective memories? The sensations of familiarity provide sense of homecoming.

The contests conclude at 6:00 P.M. The winning groups in each category are awarded their prizes: solar-powered cassette recorders, money, and instruments. Samp (cracked corn, a staple in the Zulu diet) and beans are served out of enormous caldrons. I am asked to dine at a special table reserved for honored guests. Samp and beans cooked with goat; cabbage; rice; chicken stew; squash; and a drink similar to Kool-Aid are in pots and bowls on the table. I eat reservedly—mostly vegetables—and refrain from drinking. I'm not sure about the source of the water. After dinner, the *amakosi* take their leave. The women begin to clean up and I walk back to my new home. It has been a glorious day.

Chapter 5: iNkosi

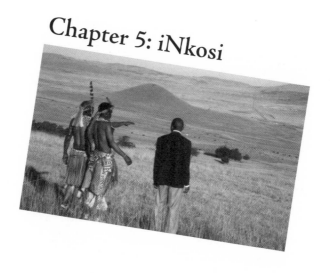

THE ZULU CULTURE SUPPORTS a king, princes, and *amakosi*, or tribal chiefs. Three hundred and fifty *amakosi* rule 6 million Zulus. Each iNkosi governs a separate tribal area. iNkosi Mazibuko heads the Mangwe-Buthanani tribe. I never hear anyone call iNkosi by a given name, he is always addressed only by his title. Our iNkosi is an unusual blend of progressive liberalism, traditional Zulu culture, self-interest, wisdom, courage, integrity, and timidity. He came to his position late in life and had no training or mentoring to assume the role as tribal leader. This role got his father and uncle, and most likely several other family members, killed, and causes his life to be threatened on more than one occasion while I am in the village.

When iNkosi Mazibuko was five years old, his father, the reigning iNkosi of the Mangwe-Buthanani, was murdered (a common means for Zulu transfer of power) and his uncle, who was thought to be the murderer, assumed the title. The heir's existence jeopardized the new lineage, putting the future iNkosi's life in danger. To protect him, iNkosi's mother fled with her children. iNkosi's uncle was later murdered, leaving the tribe without a royal leader.

In 1997, the tribe, encouraged by Amafa, voted to pursue tourism development in the area. The tribal leaders, many of whom were illiterate, believed a better-educated and more urbane person was needed to lead the initiative. They approached the then-thirty-four-year-old heir who, for the previous ten years, had worked as a policeman in Ladysmith, a town two hours away. They asked Mr. Mazibuko to return to the village and accept his rightful position as iNkosi. It was no small request. The job of iNkosi offered a greater threat to his life than did his job as a policeman. iNkosi told me that he spent time in prayer and consulting family members and political advisors before accepting the title. His mother was opposed to the offer, but the royal family pressured him. iNkosi said, "I chose to accept my destiny. I put my faith and trust in God's hands. If I must die, I accept it."

Maggie first met iNkosi during negotiations to build the lodge. All land in the tribal area is communally owned. Families have permission to occupy specific sites, but the land itself is not theirs. Maggie and Pat negotiated a deal with the tribal council to build on the land. In return, the tribal council could appoint a director of the lodge and the tribe would receive a percentage of its profits. During that process, Maggie became quite impressed with iNkosi's wisdom, integrity, and leadership potential. She understood the importance of having an intelligent and progressive leader to guide the growth of this community. In the summer of 1999, The WILD Foundation, through a grant from Maggie, sponsored iNkosi's attendance to a six-week program at Shenandoah University in Virginia designed to train leaders from developing countries in democracy, business, English, and computers. He was at the top of his class.

When I visited Isandlwana in September 1999, iNkosi was commuting from Ladysmith, four hours round-trip, after his shift on the police force. Trying to fill his role as a new iNkosi and keep his job on the police force kept him sleepless and on the road in his marginally functional car, not to mention frequently absent when needed to attend meetings in the village. iNkosi's full-time presence and active support were required if we were to attain our goal of creating economically viable, environmentally responsible programs.

The position of iNkosi did not supply an income. Maggie very generously provided a grant that enabled him to quit his job in Ladysmith. Now we would have his full-time attention, but we still faced the problem of a place for him to stay. When iNkosi and his immediate family moved from the area, they forfeited their tribal homestead. iNkosi was married with four children ages four to thirteen years. He lived without a phone sixty miles from the tribal area, a less-than-ideal situation. Once again, Maggie came to the rescue, with an offer to build him a home in the tribal area. Managing the construction of the house was part of my job. Little did I know that process would immerse me in a cross-cultural communications nightmare.

In our first meeting, iNkosi is very candid with me, a trait I later learn is extremely rare among Zulus and one that I will not again experience from him for a long time. He confides that his people are mostly good, but if they believe I take sides in local politics, they might kill me or "burn me out." He cautions that I must be very careful to remain impartial in my dealings with the tribe. I take his comments seriously.

Shortly after I move into the area, I get a taste of his position in the community. It is the day of the anniversary celebration of the Battle of Isandlwana. WILD donates seventy-five kilograms of samp and beans for the festivities. Early that morning, iNkosi arrives at my house accompanied by the tribal secretary, Miss Elizabeth Dlamini, and two members of the tribal council. I show my visitors into the living room and offer them a seat. Miss Dlamini translates. We exchange a few pleasantries. No one explains the purpose of the visit. Perhaps they've come for the samp and beans? I tell iNkosi that the samp and beans are in the kitchen, come and see. He doesn't budge. I repeat myself and add a hand gesture for emphasis. He still doesn't budge. Why isn't he moving? Maybe he needs to maintain a royal posture around councilmembers. I surmise that protocol requires me to bring the samp and beans to him.

I walk into the kitchen, pick up a fifteen-kilogram (thirty-three-pound) packet, carry it into the living room, and lay it on the floor if front of him, an offering for the chief. Without getting up, iNkosi and the councilmembers admire the samp and beans and ask how many more packets are in the kitchen. Four. They say they will need them all. No one budges. I walk back into the kitchen and return with another packet. At this point Miss Dlamini stands up, walks into the kitchen with me, and carries one of the packets into the living room. When seventy-five kilos of samp are stacked at the feet of the men, they get up, walk to the door, thank me profusely for WILD's contribution, and point toward a pickup truck. Miss Dlamini says that we—she and I—need to load the samp and beans into the truck.

I think for a second about how to handle this situation. Do I establish my authority or continue with this exercise in Zulu etiquette? The men know it is not the custom among whites for women to carry heavy loads. It feels like a test. I'm still in the early days in Isandlwana, so I go along with Zulu custom: all work is women's work. Miss Dlamini and I each pick up a packet of samp and beans and carry them out to the rusted, slightly dilapidated truck. Oh, goody! They brought the rest of the celebratory lunch. A goat and several chickens are in the back of the truck on their way to the stew pot. It's more intimacy with my food supply than this city girl wants. I heave the packet into the truck, causing an outcry from the assembled protein sources. Miss Dlamini and I finish loading the samp and beans, all egos in tact.

During my fact-finding days, I discovered that Zulu women do most of the work while Zulu men sit around. Historically, Zulu warriors protected the women and children, fought the wars, hunted game, and, in return, were cared for by women. With no more wars to fight and all the game gone, the men who remain in the area are culturally and literally jobless. Alienated and disempowered, they drink.

One South African said if I invested ten cents in a Zulu woman I would get a dollar in return; if I invested ten cents in a Zulu man, I would get ten cents of "filtered" beer in return. Harsh comments painted with too broad a brush, but definitely based in truth. iNkosi knows that if the jobs we create are given to the men, as is tradition, most of the wages will be spent on beer. Disregarding tradition and showing his progressive nature, he insists that a minimum of 40 percent of the jobs be given to women, believing their wages will be used to provide necessities for their families. Feminism at its most basic.

iNkosi is a very private man. To this day, after working closely with him for three years, I am not sure who the "real" iNkosi is. He pays close attention, learning many things through thoughtful observation. For example, he loves to use English idioms or expressions and finds appropriate occasions to say such things as, "I think that horse is already out of the barn" or "We will cross the bridge when it comes." Just about the time I think I know who he is, who I am dealing with, he surprises me. He genuinely respects women, their intelligence, talents, and the role they carry in Zulu culture. He knows that for his people to survive, the women will have to participate more actively in the decision-making process. He is committed to placing women on the tribal council. When dealing with the constant political and economic issues that challenge his authority, iNkosi will thoughtfully and intelligently work through a problem and formulate a wise and sophisticated evaluation of the situation.

The challenge comes when it is actually time to initiate a plan. Before everything else iNkosi is a Zulu steeped in a long tradition of avoidance behavior. Don't rush, if you hit a road-block, wait, don't make waves, just sit, don't move, and eventually the obstacle will move or be moved. Mountains eventually erode. He is great at saying he will do something and months later, it is not done. I am frequently left wondering if it isn't done because he doesn't want to do it, it isn't appropriate to do but he is "too polite" to tell me, he tried to do it and couldn't get it done, or he is waiting for something else to fall into place.

Despite his ability to sidestep implementation, one incident stands out in which iNkosi shows uncharacteristic initiative. The houses eventually constructed for iNkosi and WILD are sited on abandoned cornfields. They are designed to look architecturally appropriate, painted concrete simulates mud bricks, but on the fallow cornfields, they stick out like the proverbial sore thumb. The plan, which I discuss with iNkosi, is to plant trees around both houses to soften their visual impact.

Without being asked to do so, iNkosi obtains trees from a governmental nursery. The small trees arrive wrapped in black plastic sheaths, ready to be planted. I am thrilled. A few days later I notice the trees are gone. iNkosi is traveling, so I ask Miss Dlamini why the trees have been removed. She tells me the royal family insists that iNkosi not plant the trees. It is a belief among Zulus that once a tree grows taller than the headman's house he will die. No trees for our iNkosi.

There is a second part to the tree-planting saga. Much to iNkosi's credit, he attends most of WILD's workshops. He wants to be familiar with our projects so he can explain our activities if asked, and he enjoys them. Also, he knows his participation encourages others. A major focus of the training in our perma-culture gardening workshops is the importance of trees. Trees are vital for water conservation, to prevent soil erosion, for their fruit, as a habitat for birds, to provide shade for the hardworking garden-ers, and to produce life-giving oxygen. Learning this reinvigorates iNkosi's commitment to plant trees. He reorders them, and this time they are planted. The courage of one's convictions can be expressed in a variety of ways.

iNkosi is a master at knowing how to say what one wants to hear and, in the time-honored Zulu way, getting what he wants done by outlasting others' resistance. Alternatively, he also excels at getting others to do the "dirty work" and, if the plan fails, deny-ing involvement. I, more than once, am caught in that trap. One incident that leaves a particularly bad taste in my mouth involves the lodge. A man working at the lodge is known for his poor atti-tude toward the staff. The staff complains to iNkosi, and then iNkosi comes to me with their complaints, hoping I will encour-age Maggie to encourage Pat to remove him. I don't much care for this man and think the place better off without him, so with iNkosi's encouragement, I start a little e-mail campaign to let the appropriate people know that this man needs to go. The situa-tion blows up in my face. When Pat confronts the staff, they deny complaining about the man; when she confronts iNkosi, he denies complaining about him. I become a serious persona non grata at the lodge. This scenario is played out frequently in Zululand: sidestep potentially awkward or dangerous interactions, work from behind the scenes, and if it doesn't happen the way you were hoping, say, "Who, me?" I know that in this culture confrontation can cost you your life, but I still don't like it.

A situation occurs late in my stay in South Africa that illustrates the fine edge on which iNkosi's life balances. In an effort to educate and encourage iNkosi's understanding and participation in environmental conservation, we sponsor his attendance at the 7th World Wilderness Congress held in November 2001 in the South African city of Port Elizabeth. While attending the congress, iNkosi receives death threats delivered via text messaging on his cell phone: ancient behaviors combine with modern technology. One text message accuses iNkosi of being owned by the whites and going to Port Elizabeth to sell tribal land to them for profit. Another threatens his life for betraying his people. iNkosi believes the messages are from a family member trying to discredit him, thus enabling the rival family member to take power. iNkosi, understandably shaken, leaves the congress to return home where he will be seen governing his people and distancing himself from whites.

iNkosi must walk in two worlds, not alienating either culture while trying to merge the best of both. Not an easy task given people's reluctance to compromise their cultural perspective, but he is a leader willing to try.

Chapter 6:
Getting to Know You

IT IS CUSTOM FOR ZULUS to greet each other when they pass. The greeting is *saubona*, "I see you," meaning "I acknowledge your presence." The reply is *yebo, saubona*, "Yes, I see you"; *unjani*, "how are you?"; or *siyaphila* or *sikhona*, "fine," or "doing well." For a woman who spent eleven years living in New York City where one never makes eye contact with people on the street, greeting everyone I pass does not come naturally. The locals enjoy teaching me manners. If I pass a person, no matter how far off the road or trail they are, and do not greet them, I will hear a greeting shouted at my back, "*Saubona*, Carol." I jerk my head up, look around, and shout back, "*Yebo saubona*," a little embarrassed and a little annoyed that my reverie has been disturbed. They smile back and wave, knowing that they got me. I have a lot of adapting to do.

iNkosi understands the importance of gradually introducing me to the tribal community. They need time to get used to the idea of a white American woman living and working with them, and I need time to even begin to understand their customs and concerns. My experiences in Boulder, particularly the one and a half years I took off after my entrepreneurial venture, tempered my pace, but enough of a let's-get-it-done mentality remains that my early days here proceed at a frustratingly slow pace.

At community meetings, I act as an observer only. If lucky, someone speaks English and periodically summarizes the proceedings for me. If not, after the meeting ends, iNkosi explains the outcome. I become familiar with issues regarding garden sites, fences, goats damaging crops, and the ubiquitous communication snafus—a never-ending challenge in a place with no phones, cars, or roads, and a cultural propensity for indirectness. I fill the rest of my time with reading, e-mail correspondence, cooking, cleaning, trips to town, and maintaining my infrastructure. Water pumps are always broken, telephones down, generators on the blink, and batteries dead.

For the first few weeks, Beatrice is my only visitor. I suppose the rest of my neighbors are either too shy or too uncomfortable to stop by. One afternoon, about three weeks into my stay, two thirteen-year-old girls knock on my open door. With downcast eyes and an embarrassed smile, one girl asks in broken English if I will please help with their English assignments. I gladly say yes. Their names are Khati and Thendi. We use gestures, mime, a Zulu-English dictionary, and a lot of laughing to communicate. The help with English is more of an excuse than a reason. The girls are curious about the American woman who lives in their tribal area.

I play country-western and popular music from the 1960s through the 1980s on my battery-powered CD player. The CD selections betray my age, but the girls don't mind. They aren't current with Billboard's latest Top Ten. One day I bring the CD player onto the front porch where we can dance. The girls teach me Zulu dance steps, I show them, to the best of a fifty-year-old's ability, American dancing. People gather to watch, but no others participate. The girls visit regularly. One day while sitting on the front porch talking, Khati reaches up and tentatively touches my hair then quickly pulls back her hand. It is the first time she has touched a white woman's hair. I tell her it's okay and let her run her fingers through my shoulder-length locks. She is startled at how fine and soft my hair is in comparison to her wonderfully shorn woolly head. She tries to braid it and is surprised and frustrated as the braids fall out as soon as she lets go.

An interaction with staff at the lodge again highlights how very isolated this area is from the outside world. On one of my visits to the lodge, several lodge employees are gathered around the front desk.

A waitress asks, "You come from America?"

"Yes."

"Where is America and how you get here?"

I draw a crude map of the world on a piece of scrap paper and show them the relative locations of America, England, and Africa. I describe an airplane and its size in relationship to the large main room of the lodge. I tell them the airplane holds more than 300 people and that it takes fifteen hours to fly from the United States to Johannesburg. It only takes one hour to fly from Durban to Johannesburg. I can see from their expressions that they doubt my story. On my next trip into town, I buy a map of the world. I take it to the lodge and suggest that when a tourist from another country visits the lodge, they put a pin on the map in that country. The suggestion is met with blank stares. More explanation is needed.

I explain that the shapes on the map represent all the different countries in the world and where each country is in relationship to the others. I point out the southern African countries that they know. More blank stares. They have no conceptual framework for looking at maps. They have never seen a map. What they do seem to comprehend is the comparative size of America and South Africa to England.

"That little thing there—it is England?"

"Yes."

"Sho! No! How can be? How a place so small own so much? English people be very clever."

"That little country own all America?" asks a gardener.

I reply, "England hasn't owned America for more than 200 years."

"Sho! You say. When that happen? England no longer have America?"

"No, England doesn't own America."

"Bill Clinton from America, yes?"

"Yes."

"He get big trouble for relation with worker?"

"Yes. How do you know that?"

"From radio—I remember. Very silly so much talk."

An interesting perspective on information flow.

I brought Mac, my seventy-five-pound, black, curly-coated retriever love muffin of a dog with me to South Africa. In Boulder, dog ownership is a large part of the culture. Children are raised to be socially responsible; dogs are raised to be obedient and indulged. I trained Mac in Humane Society obedience classes. I dedicated time to train him the way a mother might set aside time to read to her child. Consequently, Mac is extremely well behaved. Danie and Linda are a wonderful support during my first year in South Africa. They kindly keep Mac for me while I settle into the village. Mac has their two young boys and four other dogs to play with while adapting to new surroundings. Danie says Mac is better behaved than their children. I take his compliment seriously and feel duly self-congratulatory.

Bringing Mac to South Africa may sound like folly, but it actually turns out to be a very good thing. The logistics of transport are a nightmare, but at least Mac doesn't have to be quarantined. I fill out stacks of forms: forms for the airlines, forms for the South African duty officers, and forms for the South African Department of Agriculture. I pay for special lab tests, air freighting his blood to the Centers for Disease Control in Atlanta to test for diseases that don't exist in the United States. Ah, the joys of bureaucracy. One of my concerns, once I decide to bring him to South Africa, is that upon my return I won't be allowed to bring him back into the United States. The U.S. Department of Agriculture informs me that Mac is a U.S. citizen traveling on my passport and, as such, is free to come and go from the United States at will. All he needs to return is a current rabies vaccine and proof of his origination in the United States. How cool is that? American pet owners, congratulate your pets on their citizenship!

Dogs are common in the tribal area. They are used for hunting and as alarm systems. Zulus don't name their dogs. A particular shout gets the dog's attention, or a rock thrown at the dog indicates when a behavior is unacceptable. Like quasi-feral dogs in most developing countries, Zulu dogs are twenty-five to forty pounds, in variations on brown, with short coats and airplane-wing ears. Shortly after I move to Isandlwana, but before I bring Mac home, my reading is disturbed by the sounds of snarling, barking, and yelping. I watch through my window in horror as a pack of dogs viciously attacks a cowering young pup. People on the street ignore the fracas. The pack abandons the target of the attack after they inflict several nasty bites. When I ask Beatrice about the dogfight and the observers' response—or lack thereof—she answers with relative indifference that dogs must sort themselves out. Mac doesn't stand a chance on the street here.

The young dog victimized by the pack becomes Mac's only dog friend in the area. Unlike most Zulu dogs, who are a neurotic combination of aggression and skittishness, this dog is a docile, needy animal. He approaches all people crouched low in a very submissive posture, begging for attention and food. Carol's personal survival rule: do not feed the neighborhood dogs. The supply of these half-starved feral animals rife with disease is endless. I don't want to risk a bite to me or Mac, so I toughen my heart and try to ignore them—except for this one.

Around the village, he follows a few paces behind me, always submissive with sad, pleading eyes. He peers at me through the bars of my locked security gate. He sleeps on my front porch at night. In the morning he greets me with belly low and head turned upward: *feed me.* I feed Mac as this emaciated mongrel looks on. My heart aches; I can't ignore him any longer. I pour dog food into a dish and take it out to him. He never again voluntarily leaves my side. Full-body contact is his specialty. As soon as I walk outside, there he is, standing on my feet, leaning against my leg. I name him Velcro. After a year in the village, I return from a trip to Durban to find Velcro missing. Nobody knows where he has gone—nobody seems to care. I bless him on his journey to the great beyond or to a new home.

The first time I take Mac for a walk, kids descend from the hills to follow. They trail behind, huddling together giggling and goading each other to approach. I don't want the children to be afraid of him, but for my safety, I want to maintain the illusion that Mac is a guard dog. I stop and give Mac the command to sit, stay. I walk away and leave him sitting; the children back off in fear. After a moment, I call Mac to me and give him a hand signal to sit. The children are wide-eyed at his performance. I offer Mac my hand to shake. When Mac obediently offers his paw, the children cheer, clap, and dance around. It is a celebration. I tell the children they can shake his hand too.

The push-pull of desire versus dread is acted out as children shove each other forward, daring one another to touch Mac while cowering behind bushes or each other. I hold Mac by the collar, encouraging the children to come close. One brave child moves forward to touch his back then races away as soon as his fingers come into contact with Mac's wonderfully soft coat. Adults tease me that Mac is a Zulu dog, his short, curly black hair resembling their own. People routinely approach me asking to trade food or tools for him. I always respond warmly saying Mac isn't for sale.

I become the pied piper of Isandlwana. The moment I leave my house for a walk with Mac, children appear like ants to a picnic. As the weeks progress, more children step forward to touch Mac. I show them how he can fetch a stick or a ball. They are entranced. Once the children become more comfortable around him, a young girl takes the dare and shakes Mac's paw. He gently bows his head, tenderly licking her hand. That breaks the ice. With giggles and grins, the children line up. Over the course of the next year, my patient, loving dog shakes hundreds of Zulu hands.

During one of Mac's handshaking performances, a teenage girl who speaks a little English says, "Your dog is most clever dog in world!"

"Why do you say that?"

"Missus, only very clever people speak English and your dog, he speaks English. How he learn English?"

All I can do is smile and nod. I never stop being surprised at how the tribal people process information. I use the conversation as an opportunity to expand her horizons.

"There are very many clever and well-educated people who do not speak English. They speak Japanese, German, Spanish, and many other languages."

Polite to a fault, she will not say what her body language expresses: you are teasing me, that can't be true; and she courteously walks away.

++++

My social life in the village is minimal. Evenings are the most lonely. During the day, I am out and about, attending meetings, checking on the progress of projects, and using my legs as telephone wires. Let your fingers do the walking—ha! In this village, your feet do the dialing. But at night it isn't safe to be out, even for the local people. Few women walk the roads. On the infrequent occasions that I plan to stay at the lodge after dark, I drive, even though it is a reasonable walk from my house. Another tourist lodge is about twenty miles away over isolated dirt roads. The owners graciously extend invitations to me, but I limit my visits to daylight hours. I don't want to be on the roads at night. Carjacking is a national sport.

I have no radio or TV. I don't want them. But nine months into my stay the evening isolation becomes too much. I buy a TV and a satellite dish. I am so tired of being alone reading and writing that reruns of *The Waltons* and *Star Trek* are a comfort.

For lack of anything else to do, I frequently go to bed at an embarrassingly early hour. I love mornings—getting up early is easy—but I don't like to turn on my generator before light. It is offensively noisy, and I don't want to disturb my neighbors. The noise disturbs me! In the early hours before dawn, I live by candlelight. It is wonderfully romantic to read in bed or type e-mails on my battery-powered laptop in their warm glow.

One morning I am awake at 4:00 A.M. I want a cup of tea. The floor is cold and drafty. I leave the candles on my desk and walk to the bedroom to retrieve my slippers. As I don the first slipper, my toes make contact with a wriggling mass. Unable to see and startled by the sensation, I fling the slipper at the wall while making a ridiculous squealing noise, arousing Mac. A creature flies out of the slipper and lands near my feet. Streaking to my defense, ready to protect me against all harm, Mac corners the alien entity. I take a moment to gain my equilibrium and retrieve a candle. I am embarrassed to see that the alien is actually a walnut-sized baby toad; thank goodness it isn't a scorpion. In that light and at that hour, it might as well have been an extraterrestrial. I scoop up the little toad and pitch it out the window.

With my heart pounding, still slightly dazed, I walk into the kitchen to fix tea. I don't know if intuition or divine guidance intervenes, but I lift my head just in time to confront a hideous monster dangling midair about one inch from my eyes. It is a spider the diameter of a softball hovering in the center of the kitchen. My heart, not fully recovered from the toad incident, ceases to beat for a moment. I don't know why I didn't pass out. Refusing to be outdone by my environment, I stagger backward, fumble around for matches, light a few more candles, pick up a broom, say, "Sorry, Buddy," and smash its Halloween-sized body to mush. All of those fancy, ridiculously expensive cardiac stress labs are completely unnecessary if one communes with nature.

++++

I am frequently asked if I've made friends and socialized with the tribal members. I become very fond of many, but for me the cultural divide is too wide to create true friendship. Perhaps I use too limited a definition of friends. In my world, friends, as separate from acquaintances or business associates, are limited in number but vastly important in sustaining me. They understand who I am, share similar interests, know my strengths and limitations, and love and council me through the ups and downs of life. All people share some common interests and concerns, and I can connect with the tribal members on that level, but my life experiences are so foreign to theirs that we cannot relate intimately.

Plus, there is the ever-present issue of boundaries. Requests for material or financial endowments, frequently from off my back, never cease. Give me your hat, give me money, give me your watch. If I invite young people into my house, inevitably one or more gets curious and starts opening drawers, pulling papers out of files, and inspecting the clothes in my closet. Although I understand the motivation, I am not comfortable with the behavior and even less comfortable with asking them to stop. Once in my home, with available water, warmth, and tea, some are very reluctant to leave. After hours of strained conversation, I tell them I have to work. I choose to limit interaction.

Additionally, I am uncomfortable with issues of sanitation. If invited into the homes of my neighbors and offered food or beverage, it is rude to refuse. Cholera, parasites, and other readily transmittable diseases are abundant in the area, and I desperately want to avoid contamination. I still shudder to recall my close encounter with cholera. Miss Dlamini and I visit the chairperson of one of the community gardens to check on the garden's progress. We respectfully wait outside her *rondaval*. Miss Dlamini explains that the chairperson's two-year-old grandson just died of cholera and she is preparing his body for burial. I wince at the thought of her chore. She emerges from the *rondaval* wiping her hands on a very dirty apron and then offers her hand to me in greeting. Horrified but unable to refuse, I shake it. I stare at my hand, potentially coated with cholera, with no water to clean it.

For the next few hours, I carefully avoid touching any part of my body or clothes, mentally noting the items I am compelled to touch—the door handle on my truck, the steering wheel, and my kitchen doorknob. At home, I quickly wash my hands, change my clothes, and wash my hands again. I wipe alcohol across all of the surfaces I have touched. I later learn that other members of the chairperson's family contracted cholera. Fortunately, I have the knowledge and resources to avoid the illness; many members of the community do not.

The stupefying level of HIV/AIDS demands another layer of caution in dealing with anyone who has open or bleeding cuts or sores. A lack of health care funds, combined with a fear of the diagnosis, precludes HIV/AIDS testing. Even if diagnosed, the health care system is unable to provide more than rudimentary palliative treatments. The incidence of lung ailments, skin lesions, and gastrointestinal complaints among tribal members suggests a high underlying HIV infection rate. The possibility of contracting a serious secondary infection is pervasive, especially with inadequate water for proper hygiene. These concerns keep me more isolated still.

Chapter 7: Getting Started

IN MARCH 2000, TWO MONTHS INTO MY STAY, Vance arrives to check on initial project developments. He comes toting South African dignitaries and WILD benefactors and associates. Some WILD associates, surprised by my background, question Vance and me, clearly concerned about my suitability for the position. They learned that I have never lived in Africa, I don't speak Zulu, I have never worked for a conservation or humanitarian nonprofit, and I am not trained in community development. When asked why he accepted me, Vance responds that I had worked in difficult, intense, problem-solving occupations, was obviously willing to accept change in my life, and had survived in challenging environments. He wanted a pioneer, not someone with preconceived notions ready with the usual answers. Only a brave or very insightful man would have taken me on. He is both.

At first, I am taken aback by the question; I don't have a good answer. On reflection I realize that my life shares an important commonality with the Zulus: overcoming the disempowerment of women. No program for this village, not an increase in jobs or improvement in health care or education, will be sustainable without the active participation of women. Women mold the children and direct the course of social change. I can help them assume their rightful and necessary place. Another lesson I've learned that will be invaluable is to not judge others for their choices. Goodness knows, I have made some rather poor decisions. Through that process, I learned to look to the motivation behind the choice and worked to shift that rather than simply damning the action. My training may not be formal "book learning," but I'm ready.

Vance's arrival changes the pace of my life dramatically. Vance has worked in southern Africa for twenty-five years, is well known and well respected. His friend and mentor Dr. Ian Player accompanies him. Dr. Player's many accomplishments include his pivotal role in saving the white rhino from extinction. Speaking of rhino, Vance's work pace would kill one. Vance is always on the go: organizing, networking, collaborating, and advising. Sleep is optional. I am adapting to my slow, frequently lonely pace when it whiplashes into eighteen-hour days of strategizing and formulating plans on how to proceed with the program. Although blessed by interesting, intelligent people to talk to, plan with, and be inspired by, I must admit that by the time Vance leaves I am exhausted and ready to have those white people with their ridiculous schedules gone.

The program focus becomes clear. Before educating the tribal members about nature conservation, we have to help with their immediate needs. We discuss jobs and training, sort of a chicken-and-egg debate. Training comes with the expectation of a job. What happens when people are trained but there are no jobs? Joblessness is demoralizing and the perfect recipe for trouble. It creates apathy and anger, leading to violence. Many of the teenagers in the area refuse to go to high school. Why pay school fees and buy school uniforms if there are no jobs when they graduate? But without a skill or education, how can they get a job?

The tribal area has very few jobs: eight at the visitors center, about ten jobs at the lodge, and a few more working for Amafa. Not exactly enough to sustain a community of 17,000. The absence of working-age men in the tribal area is glaringly apparent. Under apartheid, men in rural areas were relocated to work in industrial development zones and mines. Their families were left behind. This one act by the government totally restructured Zulu society. Women became heads of households. Zulu men established second families at their work sites. The men were under no legal obligation to send money back to the families they left behind. Welfare payments are essential for the survival of communities like this one.

At the end of Vance's visit, we have specific plans in place and people in agreement with our methods and goals. With no modern infrastructure and an unskilled labor force, attracting industry is almost impossible. We have to create our own means of support, building on what exists: tourism and agriculture. The Zulus need to create their economic future rather than feel alienated and disempowered waiting for handouts. Entrepreneurial endeavors seem to be the only viable solution. We will build on the skills they already have, skills that can be developed into businesses. Skill improvement and entrepreneurial start-ups have fairly long lead times before bearing palpable economic benefit. We want to start with a project that has an immediate positive impact on the lives of the people. We want to demonstrate that we are not here with empty promises, we are here to produce results.

Zulus use cattle as currency and as an indicator of wealth.

Traditionally, Zulu men pay *lobola*, bride price, to the family of their intended. On average, *lobola* is eleven cattle, but can go as high as twenty cattle if the bride-to-be is the daughter of a royal family member or especially beautiful or gifted. Any cow, no matter how sick or old, can be used. Zulu cattle procreate at their leisure with no veterinary attention or proper breeding practices. The herds have little actual economic value, but their collective numbers are in excess of the carrying capacity of the land. The overgrazed fields suffer staggering levels of topsoil erosion, which decreases the viability of the land even further. If the cycle is not stopped, the land will become incapable of sustaining any agricultural enterprise.

The erosion gullies, called *dongas*, are big—big enough to lose a truck in—and getting bigger every day. On the battlefield, erosion threatens historic gravesites. Amafa wants to protect the graves, so they agree to match funds with WILD in a soil reclamation project. Amafa hires an expert to train tribal members in erosion control techniques, then hires the tribal members to build the necessary structures to help the land repair itself. It is a win-win situation for all. The graves are protected from erosion, people receive training in a usable skill allowing for possible future employment, and the workers receive income. iNkosi wisely suggests that we rotate tribal members in teams, each working two weeks out of the three-month program so that the benefits, although meager, will assist 240 families.

Tribal policy requires that all people employed in the tribal area be selected by the tribal council rather than by the employer. This policy has pluses and minuses. It allows for a distribution of employment across all tribal wards, saves the employer the hassle of locating and communicating with potential employees, and, in theory, allows the most needy to get the jobs. The downside is favoritism: available jobs frequently going to the same few people, always the men. iNkosi prevails with his declaration that 40 percent of the jobs go to women.

The erosion control work consists of hauling rocks and dirt to build check dams in the *dongas* and roadside gullies so that, over time, they will refill with soil. Zulu women, trained from infancy to carry loads, take to the manual labor. When I walk out onto the battlefield to survey the progress, I am greeted with smiles and waves, each worker thanking me for this opportunity to work. How many women in America would be thrilled to have a summer job hauling rocks all day in blazing heat? This project puts The WILD Foundation on their map, so to speak. A year later, I notice small stone check dams constructed in some of the erosion gullies around the tribal area. The people took their training and put it to work in their own backyards. I am elated.

Even more basic than economic opportunity is the community's need for potable water. Water is supplied by a few hand pumps at boreholes scattered throughout the four-mile-wide by eleven-mile-long tribal area. Those who live far from a pump take surface water from springs or drainage ditches contaminated by parasites and other waterborne infections. Women and children carry large jugs of water up to two miles just to maintain survival allotments. The first time I see a young girl about ten or eleven years old with a sixty-pound jug of water on her head I want to scream child abuse. I can barely pick up the containers. These girls, with the help of a friend, heave the jugs onto their heads and with their arms bent backward at the elbow, balance the jug, and slowly walk home.

I talk to myself a lot during my stay. Talking to myself keeps me from saying things that shouldn't be said. I have no right to judge. I am here to help, not criticize. Maybe if we can get water closer to the homesites the girls won't have to carry so much, maybe if the families had a little more money they could afford a wheelbarrow. We can't solve all their problems, but with focus and insight we can make a positive difference.

I contact an engineering construction firm that specializes in rural water projects. After a little sweet talk, dangling the possibility of American money (shame on me), the firm agrees to conduct a water survey of the tribal area. Although the South African government has a legislative mandate to supply clean water for every South African, there are no funds available to do so. If this village is going to have more clean water anytime soon—meaning in the next two years—funding will have to come from outside. I have to raise money.

On the surface, that may not seem like such a big deal. For me it is a huge deal. I am sure a therapist reading this would have a field day analyzing my complexes around fund-raising. I hate it. It makes me feel like a beggar, like a failure, pleading with other people to help me do what I think is important but don't have the resources to do myself. I fear that if I put my emotions and values on the line and others don't respond, I am being rejected or criticized. I spent ten years on Wall Street selling stocks. Some people believe that is the same thing as fund-raising: persuading people to buy a stock is no different than persuading a person to give money for a cause. I cannot explain my dislike of fund-raising and I cannot defend it, but in the grand scheme of things, it is not too horrible a burden to carry. Despite this irrational resistance, I believe so strongly in the vital right of every human being to have sufficient potable water that I write a letter of solicitation:

March 25, 2000

Dear Friends and Family,

There is a glaring need in this community for adequate, safe water. These rare and precious people are struggling to retain their powerful and proud traditions while being forced to survive in a world that was not made for them or by them, but nonetheless inherited and now under their authority. From numerous environmental, cultural, and political changes, this rural traditional Zulu village finds itself without an adequate water supply.

The community is under the rule of a young, progressive, educated, and very dedicated leader. Seventeen thousand people inhabit a 100-square-kilometer area with no piped water, phones, or electricity, and other than a small amount of tourism, no industry. Initiatives to improve the local economy are dependent on creating a supply of adequate, safe water.

Water is currently supplied by hand pumps scattered throughout the community. Women and children carry large jugs of water up to two miles just to have sufficient water to cook and drink, allowing little extra for sanitation. People in homes farther from the pumps are forced to take water from springs and creeks contaminated with parasites and other waterborne infections. Water from the pumps can dry up in the winter, creating a further water shortage.

There is a massive health crisis in South Africa from HIV/AIDS. AIDS and parasitic infections compromise the immune system allowing opportunistic infections, such as tuberculosis, pneumonia, liver, kidney, and intestinal infections to take hold. Children are particularly vulnerable to these infections. Without a clean and adequate water supply, the spread of these secondary infections may result in an even worse health crisis than the AIDS epidemic is at present considered to be. A civil engineering firm donated time to evaluate the water situation.

For about $5 per person, we can bring a lifetime supply of safe water to each *muzi*, or homesite, with the substantial secondary benefit of creating temporary employment and providing income to this impoverished area.

For more than twenty-five years The WILD Foundation has gained an impeccable reputation and track record serving the environment and its most rural people. Donations are 100 percent tax deductible and all donations will go directly to support this project. Please open your hearts and your pocketbooks to help me give this gift of life and hope to these very deserving people in this place that, for now, I call home. I know we can raise the $125,000 to complete this project.

Please mail all contributions to The WILD Foundation, P.O. Box 1380, Ojai, CA 93024. Please mark checks "IS Water Project" so that the funds will be allocated appropriately. If you have any questions, you may contact Vance Martin, president of The WILD Foundation.

Thank you,
Carol Batrus

I send the letter to friends, acquaintances, and family. In the metaphysical/spiritual world there is a belief that you create your own reality—sort of a self-fulfilling prophecy. In a romanticized illusion, I believe that the people to whom I send my letter, who live half a world away and culturally hundreds of years apart, will feel my dedication and the rightness of my cause and will open up their coffers. Think again. I raise $640. Better than a poke in the eye, but far short of what I need. I believe fund-raising will be awful, and emotionally it is. My brother saves the day by sending $10,000 to support the cause. Grateful, I swear I won't expose myself like that again. One would think that at my age I would know not to say foolish things I will later defy.

Even with the additional money, we don't have nearly enough to adequately fund the project. I set the plan aside until I have more time to focus on the financing. Right now, I have projects to begin, training to initiate, and a culture to understand.

Chapter 8: Praise the Lord

I AM IN FOR THE NIGHT, WONDERING WHAT TO DO to entertain myself, when I hear a knock at my door. Beatrice invites me to a regional youth rally at the church. I quickly change clothes—I have been lounging in sweats and slippers—and follow Beatrice across the street to the church. The church overflows with Zulus fourteen to twenty years old dressed in their Sunday best. A portable generator along with amplifiers, a keyboard, and an electric guitar have been donated for the night. Traditional Zulu drums complete the band. Two hundred amazingly happy, beautiful young Zulus are gathered to praise God and rock and roll. I am the only white person in the church. Given I am the only white person in the village makes that a frequent occurrence. The kids don't bat an eye at my arrival. I join them in the aisles dancing, singing, shouting, clapping, and praising the Lord. Two boys walk over to shake my hand and dance next to me. Maybe they think that for an old white lady I don't dance too badly. Hallelujahs and amens echo in the rafters. One song for Jesus reminds me of a football cheer: give me a "j" J, give me an "e" E, give me an "s" S ... I depart around midnight, exhausted and happy. The kids party on until morning.

On April 23, 2000, I celebrate my first holiday in South Africa: Easter. The hot summer months are slipping into a mild and very pleasant early fall. Easter in the fall, Christmas in the summer; it feels very strange. The leaves on the few deciduous trees in the area are changing color. An Easter display in Dundee has Easter eggs in fall colors: tan, gold, orange, and avocado green. Dried corn stalks and squash surround them. Wait, this isn't Thanksgiving, it's Easter! The visual effect is disorienting and a bit disturbing. The traditions of Easter are the rights of spring, fecundity and new life, not harvest then decay. Another challenge to my worldview and another opportunity to expand beyond it.

On Easter morning the bell in the old wooden bell tower on the grounds of the church starts its peal, alerting the village that it is 7:00 A.M. Church begins in two hours. It is unusual for me to be in bed this late; I generally get up about 5:00, but last night I woke up and read for a while. I take full advantage of the freedom afforded by my scheduleless existence. From my bed I can see the sky through my open window. It is cloudless and sunny, already about sixty degrees. A seductive breeze caresses my face. It feels like a beautiful Colorado day. I am homesick for cool mountain air and sparkling skies. I fix tea and mealie (corn) porridge and settle down to write e-mails.

As the village stirs, animal sounds increase. Cows moo, goats bleat, and chicken squawk. Chasing off goats and chickens and shoving cows away from my driveway gate is a daily ritual. Adding to the menagerie, toads abound in April, brought out by a rain-filled summer. I am adept at shoeing toads from behind doors, under beds, and between sofa cushions. Mac is expert at herding the toads—prancing, hopping, and yelping as he noses them toward the exit.

I hear Mac's nails on the cement stoop and glance up, expecting to see him. Instead, a baseball-sized toad hops through the door into the living room and, without a pause, straight-lines into the kitchen and out the kitchen door, passing through the bars on the closed security gate. Trailing the toad, a chicken clucks and struts its way past me, following the toad into the kitchen, through the security bars, and out the door. Mac, not to be left behind, follows, but can't get through the security bars on the kitchen gate. He reverses course and runs back through the living room to catch up to his newly acquired playmates. Undisturbed by the scene, I return to my writing.

The bell tolls again, 8:00 A.M., one hour until church, or so they pretend. Church really doesn't get started until 9:30 or later. I write a little while longer, then get dressed in a skirt and blouse, the first skirt I have worn in weeks. I meet up with Cheryl, one of the new managers from the lodge, and enter the church, but no one is inside. We see the congregation gathered in the graveyard down the hill and walk down to join them. They are celebrating the resurrection of Christ. After the ceremony in the graveyard, we form a procession and enter the church.

The congregation gathers at the rear of the church around the baptismal font. Three children are christened. After the christenings, Cheryl and I are asked to sit in two chairs placed beside the front pew. I feel singled out, embarrassed, but touched that our presence is honored. A member of the Mothers Union offers Zulu hymnals and prayer books along with an English Bible for us to share. I love to sing the Zulu hymns, and it's easy if the tempo is slow. A woman sitting next to us maintains a supervising eye and points to the correct passage if we lose our place.

After four months here, Anglican sites blended with Zulu sounds feel familiar.

About one hour into the service the minister calls Cheryl and me to the front of the church. He asks us to kneel as he prays over us, blessing our work and asking the Lord to keep us safe. He prays in both Zulu and English. I am grateful for the congregation's warm welcome but am a little concerned over their expectations. This place and these people need so much; I feel ill prepared and ill equipped to provide it. I promise myself that I will do the best I can and then release both our expectations to the fates.

Cheryl and I return to our seats and listen to the Zulu sermon. At a convenient break, two hours into the service, we leave. Church will go on for many more hours. I walk back to my house, feeling content and needing to express some joy. I turn on my CD player and dance around the cottage with Mac. Mac can do a mean cha-cha—if only I could get him to stop mouthing my wrists when I hold his paws.

At 1:00, I walk up to the lodge to join Cheryl and her husband for Easter dinner. The guests have left on an all-day tour and Pat is in Durban. Most of the staff are off. The lodge feels deserted. Dinner is a cross-cultural mix, a Chinese-like chicken stir-fry coated in a South African *braai* (barbecue) sauce. Not exactly my idea of an Easter meal, but very tasty.

Afterward, since Mac and I haven't walked up the hill behind my house to watch a sunset in several days, I decide to treat myself to the view. It is a lovely, gentle evening. Clouds streak the sky with soft pastels of pink, peach, and lavender. As usual, kids gather to walk with us. They ask for sweets, but I never carry any with me. I won't support their begging.

Mac bounds toward three goats, goading them to play. The

goats don't share his enthusiasm and try to gore him. I command Mac to leave the goats alone. When he responds, I praise him in a silly baby-talk voice that I have used with him since he was a puppy. Two children covertly mimic the voice and glance questioningly at me to see if it's okay. I laugh and again praise Mac in my silly voice. They mimic my voice exactly, and dance and clap and cheer when he responds. Amazing, such simple joy. I walk home, fix tea, and read for a while. My first holiday in Zululand is, all in all, a very good day.

++++

From early colonial days, the British ruled this part of South Africa, establishing the Anglican Church as the largest religious presence but far from the only influence. The Dutch brought the Dutch Reform Church and the Germans brought Lutheranism. Many Protestant churches sent missionaries. When laborers and merchants arrived from India, they created the largest population of Indians anywhere outside of India. Even little Dundee has two Hindu temples. Eastern influence enters into Zulu cooking, adding rice and curry flavors. I want to learn about traditional Zulu religion and spirituality, but when I question Beatrice or other local women about the old beliefs, I get no answers, just shy downward glances and a change of subject. They are either unwilling to discuss religion with an outsider or so removed from their spiritual heritage that they are unable to answer my questions.

One religion spawned in Natal is the creation of a Zulu named Shembe. While driving around the rural areas, I notice large circles of white-painted stones in the fields. Beatrice tells me they are gathering sites for Shembe services. The religion is named after its founder. It is a blend of Old Testament teachings, American and European Protestant influence, with a little Muslim folded in to make for an eclectic belief system. Services are held on Saturdays. Shembe followers eat beef but no pork, and unmarried women wear white. I mention to Danie, the friend who took care of Mac when we first arrived, that I want to attend a service. He arranges for a friend and Zulu guide to take Linda, their sons, and me to a Shembe gathering.

The guide drives us to a large Shembe compound in a township north of Durban. Maneuvering Danie's four-door pickup over the narrow, winding dirt tracks is a challenge. The streets are clogged with pedestrians. At each turn, our vehicle attracts stares and curious glances. I see no white faces. This township is without the heart-wrenching poverty of the squatter shacks one sees along highways outside of major South African cities. Small shops and homes made of cinder block or plywood, actually more like sheds, line dirt roads. Vendors selling food—fruits, grilled meats of indeterminate origin, and baked products—are doing a brisk business. I can smell spoiled food and a general scent of unclean.

Our guide parks near the entrance gates of a fenced compound. We descend from the truck and are greeted by a man wearing a dark suit and carrying a prayer book. He asks that we remove our shoes and proceed barefooted. Danie must remove his hat, Linda and I must cover our heads. Thank goodness I brought a hat with me. I carry my camera but am asked to leave it in the vehicle. We walk barefoot for about a quarter of a mile across the garbage-strewn ground. Africa is not a land for sissies.

Our destination is a large grove of trees undergrown with patchy, well-worn grass. There are no chairs or benches. A square "gazebo" of beige-colored bricks stands in the middle of the trees. Lilac-colored curtains partially enclose the structure, but it is open enough to expose an empty armchair draped with lace antimacassars. Our guide tells me that the chair is a ceremonial seat for their departed founder and prophet (he died in 1935). No other whites are present. The man who greeted us collects two people from the assembled crowd. A woman escorts Linda and me to an area under the trees where women gather. A man escorts Danie and his sons to the men's area. An aisle demarcates the two sections. At the back of the aisle, an amplifier with microphone and a tape recorder rest on a table.

The women wear magnificent Queen Nefertiti-meets-Jackie O headdresses. They are pill-box shaped, but taller and flattened on top, woven from goat hair dyed brick red, and decorated with glass beads and embroidery. The men wear animal-skin headbands with animal tails hanging down their necks. All of the men have facial hair. Everyone wears Western clothes—suits or trousers and shirts on the men, skirts and blouses on the women—but no one wears shoes.

To the left of the women's section, on the far side from the men, sit a group of young virgins, totally covered as is Muslim tradition, wrapped in plain white shawls and robes. Our greeter offers to answer a few questions. He explains that in a heavily chaperoned annual event, eligible bachelors gather to view the faces of the virgins in order to select a bride. Only married women can speak to the virgins. Linda and I are offered a Zulu prayer book, a hymnal, and a grass mat. We sit with the other women on the grass mats under the trees. I have on an ankle-length, full skirt, so I feel comfortable sitting cross-legged. I am politely instructed by hand signals and example to sit with my knees together and my ankles crossed, feet placed to my right.

The minister picks up the microphone and begins the service. He speaks Zulu and no one around us speaks English; what is said remains a mystery. Linda and I watch the other women and keep pace in the hymnal. We listen, pray, and sing. Kneeling looms large. We kneel for every prayer. Kneeling on grass mats over hard ground is tough on the knees. After the service, Danie tells me that one of the prayers lasted nineteen minutes; he timed it.

When it is time for the offering, worshipers line up and walk on their knees to the offering bowl. That surpasses my comfort level. Linda and I hunch over, crouch low, and scurry our way to the offering bowl. Watching the people crawl on their knees reminds me of a favorite poem called "Wild Geese" by Mary Oliver from her book *Dream Work*. It begins: *You do not have to be good, you do not have to walk on your knees for 100 miles through the desert repenting, you only have to let the soft animal of your body love what it loves.* Apparently, they do not embrace her philosophy.

Two hours into the service, a woman motions for us to follow her. She leads us to our guide, Danie, and the boys. Time to leave. The service will go on for a while longer. I'm not sure what I expected, but it wasn't what we experienced. The impression I got from seeing the circles of stones in fields would be a service more primitive or with indigenous ritual. Once again, I am fooled by my expectations, a statement that applies to most of my life.

Chapter 9:
Safety vs. Freedom

I CONSIDER MYSELF A BRAVE rather than a timid or easily frightened person. I camp alone and travel alone. While earning my M.B.A. at Columbia, I lived in Harlem alone. I may not trust that I know what I'm doing with my life, but I have always trusted that, with a little common sense, I would be safe. When I lived in Harlem, if I was out late I took a cab home and asked the cabbie to wait at the curb until I was inside my building. When camping alone, I kept my truck keys with me so that I could leave if I felt threatened. I'm sure there are people who show an equal amount of caution yet experience violent or threatening events. Perhaps it is my destiny to feel and be safe, but no aspect of my life prepared me for the security issues that exist in South Africa.

In Johannesburg, I am startled to see that private homes are enclosed by eight-foot walls topped with barbed wire or broken glass bottles set in cement, the jagged edges menacing upward. Electric gates guard driveways, and signs announce that breaks in security bring armed response. Nearly everything has a lock on it.

Refrigerators have locks, phones have locks, closets have locks, windows have bars and locks, doors have security gates with locks. I own more keys than will fit in my pockets. There are six different keys for my truck alone: to unlock the immobilizer, gear shift, spare tire, back canopy, door, and for the ignition. I also have gate keys, house door keys, shed keys, and more. Just keeping track of all the keys is stressful. Accepting that the locks are necessary is daunting. The locks keep people out but lock me in. At all times I have to know where my keys are so I can get out in case of emergency. It is a horrible way to live.

Maintaining constant awareness of my security is exhausting. I didn't realize how exhausting until I returned from South Africa to live once again in a place where I take my safety for granted. Not needing to be ever vigilant of my surroundings and of the location of my keys (in Boulder I have only three: one for my car, one for my garage, and one for my condo) feels like a weight has been lifted.

When asked what it was like living in South Africa, if I mention issues of security the questioner inevitably becomes uncomfortable. One woman doubts my assertion that feeling unsafe was a constant drain.

"Oh, it couldn't have been that bad!"

I ask her, "How many times in a week do you worry about being raped or violently assaulted?"

"I don't."

"How many times a year do you worry about being raped or violently assaulted?"

"I don't."

"How many times in your life have you worried about being raped or violently assaulted?"

"Not many. I use common sense."

Yes, common sense. But common sense in one culture may not be common sense in another.

South Africa has the highest per capita incidence of rape anywhere in the world, and kwaZulu-Natal has the highest incidence of rape in South Africa. In Natal, rape can be a death sentence, as Natal also has the highest incidence of HIV/AIDS in South Africa. Private surveys indicate that up to two-thirds of all Zulus between the ages of eighteen and thirty-five are HIV positive. To help prevent the spread of AIDS, a group of community workers in Ulundi, the capital of kwaZulu-Natal, used the theme of Return to Traditional Values as the basis for their program. Traditionally, a girl's virginity was required to secure a good marriage and bride price. Each girl was expected to conduct herself in a manner that prevented her from being raped or seduced into intercourse. In return, the community protected and lauded these virgins. Matrons checked the women to assure their virginity was intact before offering them for marriage at the age of twenty-one. Building off that traditional expectation, the community workers initiated a Virgin Girls Clubs. The organizers hoped that the members would again be placed in positions of esteem, encouraging abstinence and suppressing the transmission of AIDS. Unfortunately, a modern-day superstition spread that having intercourse with a virgin would cure AIDS. Tragically, these girls become the target of HIV-infected rapists. The clubs were abandoned.

I hear dreadful tales—everyone has them—about rape, robbery, carjackings, and assault. South African common sense dictates that I should *never* go out alone, *never* go out at night, and *never* leave anything unlocked. When I retrieve Mac from Danie and Linda, Danie tells me that Zulus, like most Africans, are terrified of black dogs. Mac will be good protection for me but I should keep him close or he might be killed. How absurd. Who could be afraid of my gentle, loveable, goofy dog? A few days after Mac comes to live with me, Beatrice knocks on my door. Mac, as is his habit, erupts in gleeful barking, thrilled that someone has come to play. Beatrice will not enter. "I am afraid of your dog," she says.

I grab Mac by his collar and tell him to be quiet. He obeys.

"My dog is very gentle. He just wants to play."

"No—I am afraid."

I close Mac in the bedroom. Slightly embarrassed, Beatrice asks about Mac.

"How can you have a dog in the house? Doesn't he go to the toilet?"

"He knows to go outside. I trained him."

"How did you do that?"

"It's easy—I did it when he was a puppy. Dogs in America live in houses with their owners."

She looks at me with disbelief. "Why do you want your dog inside?"

"He keeps me company and he is good protection. No one can come close to the house without my knowing it. And I don't want anybody to hurt him or steal him."

"Yes—that is true. You should keep him with you. Black dogs frighten people. He could be killed."

Occasionally, Mac accompanies me on trips to town. When I walk with him, even if he is on lead, blacks cross the street or walk out into it to avoid passing us on the sidewalk. At first, I think these are isolated incidents, but after several trips to town where black pedestrians cut a wide path around us, I realize the truth in Danie's comments.

WILD provides for my security with a citizens band radio

linked to the police and a network of farms surrounding the tribal area. I have a transmitter in the house and one in my truck. In conversations with iNkosi, Vance insists that the tribe make every effort to assure my safety. iNkosi announces at a community meeting that it is the tribe's responsibility to keep me safe. I provide resources for the tribe. The tribe must protect me. Beatrice takes that mission to heart.

Early in my stay, Mac and I walk up the hill behind my house to enjoy the sunset. It is my day's last hoorah outside before locking myself inside. After four sunset strolls, Beatrice comes to my house to tell me not to walk up the hill anymore in the evening.

"Don't do the same thing at the same times. People will know and hide in wait for you. You could get hurt. It happens," she says.

I am surprised but accept her caution. The next evening I walk across the plains toward the south. I pass Beatrice's house on my return. She shouts out the window, "Wait!"

"Don't walk that way (pointing south). That is out of our tribal area to a bad place. Criminals live there. You won't be safe."

"Where is it safe for me to walk?"

"Only in this area, around the mission, up to the lodge, and on the battlefield, but only on this side of the hill where we can see you. Nowhere else."

I already feel confined; it is beginning to feel like a prison. Given the dire warnings to stay safe I acquiesce to her advice, resenting the restrictions.

Lack of local employment forced most men of the tribe to move to urban areas for work. During holidays, many husbands and extended tribal members, occasionally fleeing from the law, return. I am repeatedly warned that these men can be trouble, keep away from them. One afternoon on a holiday weekend, I linger on my walk a little too long. It is approaching dark as I near my house. Two men in their twenties with cocky, menacing swaggers fall in behind me. I am frightened. Mac is exploring in the bushes. He emerges and sees the men trailing us. True to his outlook on life, he responds as if they had come to play. With his tail whirligigging behind him, he bounds toward them.

In the blink of an eye these two bold, threatening Zulus turn tail and run as fast as they can, which I must say is impressively fast. Now the encounter has turned into Mac's favorite game: chase. Mac runs even faster. I turn to follow. I am afraid for my safety, but I am more afraid that they might hurt Mac. By the time I catch up with the fleet-of-foot, the men are cowering on top of a tin-roofed shed at the visitors center. I call Mac to me and we walk home in peace. Later, I am told that the men raped two girls before leaving the area. I am convinced that Mac, solely through his sweet black presence, protected me.

It is early April 2000. I haven't traveled outside the area. I want to explore South Africa and experience its amazing animal life. Elephants and giraffe don't exactly roam freely across the tribal plains; they were long ago eradicated by hunters. I know I shouldn't travel alone, so I phone Linda and invite her to go with me to a local game reserve—a girls' getaway weekend. The invitation surprises her. She has never spent a weekend away from family and home. "Are all American women so independent?" she asks. Women's lib and the feminist movement are in their infancy in South Africa, especially in the Afrikaner community, where women are expected to stay home and care for their families to the exclusion of other activities.

Danie supports the idea and recommends a lovely little guesthouse and restaurant near the reserve. He offers to keep Mac and encourages Linda to go. I drive to Durban to drop off

Mac and pick up Linda. We arrive at the guesthouse in the early afternoon. It is a beautiful location, set on a plateau overlooking a valley. Our room is a modernized cement *rondaval* that opens onto a common lawn with tables and flower gardens. I feel better already. We enjoy tea in the garden then drive to the game reserve. We cruise around for a while but see little. A game ranger tells us that the best times for viewing animals are sunrise and sunset. We return to the guesthouse, eat an early dinner, and plan to be at the game reserve for sunrise. After dinner, we read in our room and fall asleep about 9:30 P.M.

A commotion coming from the restaurant's bar wakes us up at 11:00. Drunks with Afrikaner accents yell for more drinks. We hear other voices trying to calm them, then ask them to leave. "No way, we want drinks," is the garbled reply. Bleary with sleep, Linda and I wonder aloud how long the disturbance will continue. A very drunk man, slurring Afrikaner-accented English, yells, "I want the Americano to come out and play." The sound of his voice moves closer as he shouts. The locked door handle to our room turns and jiggles. I scream through the door, "Go away!" The drunk responds, "Americano come out!" He continues working the door handle. I get up, turn on the light, and look for a phone to call the manager for help, but there is none. I check my cell phone. No cell coverage. I pray the lock holds. Damn it! Where is the management?

We hear voices by the door coaxing the man to move away. He slurs Afrikaner words. Linda tells me he said, "I want the woman." I move through anger into fear. The other voices convince him to go back to the bar. We hear fists pounding on wood and demands for more drinks. More drunken shouting—again he returns to our door, trying to force the lock. The lock holds. He moves to the window and pounds on the glass. I keep screaming, "Go away!" Once more, other men firmly coax him back to the bar. Linda and I believe the assault is over so I turn off the light and go back to bed. Fifteen minutes later, he returns, this time with something metal to try to pry the door and window open. Men's voices yell at him to stop, saying it is time to leave. The drunk shouts, "Come out Americano!." I scream back, "Go away!" He slurs, "Goooooo aaawaaaayyyy" and laughs. More voices tell him it is time to leave. We hear the sound of a man urinating on our window. Walking away, he shouts in Afrikaans, "I'll be back for the Americano tomorrow."

I lay in bed planning what I will say to the manager in the morning. How dare he allow this! At sunup, ready for a confrontation, I go looking for the piece of crap, prepared to express my ire with trading-floor precision. I find the manager in the restaurant preparing for breakfast. He is stooped over, setting a table, and doesn't look up when I approach him. I want to scream and swear at him, but I can't. Instead, I ask, "What happened last night?" My voice is shaky. I am near tears.

He says, "I'm sorry about last night, but at least you weren't hurt. They were local farmers who came from a shooting competition. They arrived drunk with a *bakkie* filled with rifles. I asked them to leave, but they told me if I didn't serve them they would shoot the place up. I did get them to leave their rifles in the *bakkie*. They only had their handguns with them."

I stutter, "They had guns?" my voice cracking, tears forming.
"Yes."
"Why didn't you call the police?"
"If the police ran them off, they would come back and shoot the place up."
"Why wouldn't the police arrest them?"
"They're local boys and they hadn't done anything."

The young manager looks like a frightened child. The potential consequences of gun-toting drunks trying to break into my room lands in my consciousness like a rock. I ask, my voice escalating in pitch with each syllable, "How did they know an American woman was here? How did they know my room?"

"I guess I shouldn't have said anything. I thought if they knew I had an American guest they would be quiet."

The manager is pathetic. I feel sorry for him. I return to our room and recount the tale. Linda shrugs, agreeing that the police would have done nothing, or if they ran off the drunks, they would have come back and made things worse. The manager had done the best he could. "That's the way things are," she says resignedly.

We have lost our enthusiasm for the area, but I am determined not to have our trip ruined. We change plans and drive the Midlands Meander, a tourist route that passes through a scenic part of the province filled with specialty shops and restaurants. The road signs identifying the stops are quite large and packed with listings and diagrams, but impossible for me to read while driving by. I slow down to pull off onto the shoulder of the road. Four young men in a rusted out Datsun hatchback pull up beside us. All four are leaning out the window, waving beer bottles, and shouting at us in Zulu. I can't understand what they are saying, but it doesn't sound friendly. I smile, nod politely, and motion for them to pass. Their shouting escalates, arms flailing angrily in our direction.

We roll up the windows, lock the doors and I floor the accelerator in my underpowered diesel pickup. It moans its way back onto the highway. Grinding gears, the Datsun sputters in pursuit with the passengers leaning out of the car windows and shouting. No other cars are on the road. My first instinct is to get to a crowded area for safety. I turn at the first intersection to find a shop or restaurant. The Datsun turns to follow. About 500 feet down the road, a signboard marks the entrance to a horse farm. Eyes glued to the rearview mirror, I turn into the driveway. Their car stops at the driveway entrance. One of the men throws an empty beer bottle toward us as their car proceeds past. My hands are trembling and my foot on the brake shakes uncontrollably. It is time to go home.

On the drive back to Durban, we treat ourselves to dinner at a lovely and delightfully crowded outdoor restaurant. When we arrive at Linda's home, her two young sons and my sweet dog greet us warmly. I stay the night and drive to Isandlwana the next morning. No more girls' weekends out. Three months later, while Linda is on her way to meet her sons at school, two boys who appear to be fourteen years old assault her. With a knife pointing at Linda's chest, her assailants demand her cell phone. She tells them to go away. One replies, "We *will* put the knife through your heart." She hands the boys her cell phone and continues to school to meet her sons.

South Africans, especially the women, seem to accept this level of violence. If I ask about it, they acknowledge its existence but present a front that denies its impact. "Yes, there is some violence, but it doesn't bother me," they say.

One woman comments, "I think the violence is overstated," then proceeds to tell me that once when stopped at a traffic light in Durban a man pushed a gun through her open car window, held it to her head, and told her to get out. The light changed at that moment and she sped away unharmed. Her house was broken into only twice, no one was hurt, and only once was a family member injured in an assault.

"You see, it's not so bad."

I attend a program planning meeting for the 7th World

Wilderness Congress at Shamwari, a well-guarded, elegant private game reserve. Vance asks me what I most enjoy about the location. Without pause, I reply, "Being able to be out at night and walk under the stars." My response surprises me as well as Vance. I reflect for a moment to check if my answer feels truthful—it does. Being able to feel safe outside at night is more important and more enjoyable than seeing the animals.

I have that sentiment confirmed in 2002. Margot, the wife of Vance's South Africa counterpart, Andrew Muir, visits the United States on a combined family holiday and fund-raising tour. I join them at Mrs. Bryant's in Virginia. Margot asks, "Is it really safe to go out at night?"

"Yes, you can a walk across the fields at 2:00 A.M. and be safe."

After a late evening gathering, I offer to drive her and her two children about a half mile to where they are staying.

"No, I want to walk. I want to feel what it's like to be outside at night and safe."

In the United States, I listen in despair as Americans bemoan how unsafe it has become, but I understand they do not share my perspective. People evaluate situations based on their experience. My experience tells me that I am blessedly, joyously safe.

Chapter 10:
Time, Patience, and Surrender

I LEARN A LOT during my time in Africa. I learn about coping, about people, and about how I view the world. Some lessons are superficial, some change the very essence of who I am. No lesson is more powerful than understanding my relationship with time and patience. After ten years on Wall Street, where even immediate gratification took too long, how could I, a hardworking Westerner taught that God and self-worth exist in productivity, tolerate a place where there is no sense that anything ever has to get done *now*?

As far as I can tell, there is no word in the Zulu culture that means *now*, as in immediately. "I will do it now" functionally translates to "before your children have children or maybe never." The expression "just now" means anytime later today—or tomorrow. "Now now" means within the next hour or two or maybe more. "Quickly" means faster than a snail's pace, but not so fast that your body would be disturbed by the movement. Einstein taught that time is relative, a shifting measure. Zulus embody time in its fluid form.

During my September 1999 reconnaissance trip to South Africa, I experience my first taste of Zulus' relationship to time. Sally offers to drive two Zulu dance judges from a village about forty miles from Isandlwana to a dance contest. With no phones to confirm schedules, she sets a time to meet them at a designated intersection. She is delayed and unable to notify the judges so they wait for an hour and a half by the side of the road. The judges make it to the dance contest in time because the dance program is also delayed. After the contest, Sally invites the judges to the lodge. She asks, through a Zulu interpreter, if visiting the beautiful, upscale lodge was worth the wait. The interpreter looks at her quizzically. She repeats herself and, to add clarity for the interpreter, explains about the delay in meeting the judges. The interpreter and the judges chat back and forth, clearly confused. The interpreter says he is having trouble translating the concept of "worth the wait." How can waiting be worth anything?

A year later, the theme reprises in an entrepreneurial training session. I am helping women launch start-up businesses. The women must learn to price their craft items for sale rather than have shop owners price the items. The crafters frequently receive pathetically low compensation for their products or, conversely, some crafters ask outrageous sums for what they produce, hoping that a few days' work will supply them with enough money to live on for months.

The dialogue, interpreted by Miss Dlamini, goes thusly:

Me: How many days does it take you to make this?

Crafter: That depends on what other things I have to do.

Me: If you did nothing but work on this, how long would it take you to make one?

Crafter: I can't work only on it, I have to fix meals and take care of my family.

Me: Of course, but if you could just work on it how long would it take to complete one?

Crafter: Blank stare.

••••

I try a different approach.

Me: If I supply the materials, would you make me one for ten rand?

Crafter: Yes.

Me: How many could you make in one month if you could work six to eight hours a day, six days a week on them?

Crafter: Maybe ten.

Me: Would you take a full-time job for 100 rand ($10) a month?

Crafter: No, that is not good.

Me: How much do you think is a reasonable monthly wage?

Crafter: 400 rand.

Me: Okay, that means if you make ten of these a month you have to charge forty rand more than the cost of the materials for each item.

Crafter: I could not do that, it would be too much. Ten rand is okay.

We have a lot of training to do.

Of the many and varied warnings I receive from white South Africans, the most frequent comment is that life in Zululand will require Herculean amounts of patience. My pace slows to match the tempo of my surroundings. If coworkers from my trading floor days assessed my life's pace in Boulder, they would have ordered emergency resuscitation equipment, doubting that a person could be alive while moving so slowly. Boulder's activity level, in comparison to life in Zululand, seems hectic. Here, days pass with no measurable forward movement, no decisions made, no product produced.

The first true test of my ability to exist outside Western time occurs during my second meeting with the tribal council. I arrive promptly at the designated hour, 10:00 A.M. The council meeting is in progress. Glancing through the open door, I catch iNkosi's eye to let him know I have arrived, then sit on a rock to wait. As I sit I think, "Carol, get used to this, they aren't very good with time." It is a beautiful, sunny day with a soft breeze and clouds drifting overhead. As rocks go, mine is fairly comfortable, but even so, every few minutes I look at my watch, becoming increasingly annoyed at being left waiting. I have better things to do. (I'm not sure what those things are, but don't we always have better things to do than just sit?) After a half hour, Miss Dlamini comes out of the meeting, graciously apologizes for keeping me waiting, then tells me a problem has come up and my part of the meeting is delayed. Will I please continue to wait? She will come out to get me when they are ready.

I think, "What's the big deal? I am here to work with the tribe, my time is their time. If they don't use it, no big deal. Work with them at their pace." I watch the clouds and say a little prayer for patience. I take off my watch and put it in my pocket. I find things around me to observe: ground termites building up the mound at the mouth of their home, hawks gliding on air currents, cows grazing in the distant field. "Be still, enjoy the scenery," I say to myself, "There is nothing more important than now."

Miss Dlamini emerges from the meeting and again apologizes for the delay. She explains that a councilman found a dead man by the side of the road. (I can see how that might interfere with the flow of a meeting.) Another councilman went to Nqutu, a small Zulu community about ten miles away, to notify the police. The rest of the council is going to see if they can identify the body. Will I please wait here for the council to return? It shouldn't be too long. Okay with me, it sure beats going to look at a dead body.

I recall exercises I learned from a meditation teacher. When I first tried meditation, I was unable to sit still for a single minute. I wiggled and twitched, scratched my nose and adjusted my butt. The teacher brought an egg timer and suggested I build up to five minutes. Five minutes—I could do that. The training was a revelation. I could be still and it felt wonderful. After a year, I could sit motionless comfortably and meditate for forty-five minutes, pretending time didn't exist. I see how long I can just be on the rock. I sit and sit and sit. Unable to resist I look at my watch. Three hours have passed since I arrived. I congratulate myself on sitting so well—but I am done now.

My inner monologue increases in its intensity. "This is unreasonable. How much am I supposed to take? This is absurd." I understand the concept that the present moment is the only time that is real, that being patient is a vital part of letting go of my ego needs, opinions, and personal agenda, but this is outrageous. I get up and pace, muttering to myself that enough is enough. I spy a member of the tribal council as he appears over the rise of the hill. They are returning. Miss Dlamini says they will be ready for me in a moment. (I won't hold my breath.) True to her word, within fifteen minutes she comes to get me. I do my presentation. It is 3:00 P.M. when I finish. I have passed a cosmic initiation ritual. What I don't know is that it is a level one initiation, and I have more levels to go.

Daily life in the village provides abundant, ongoing opportunities to practice patience. I attend meetings in which each participant is asked for his or her opinion. No one can simply say, "I agree with Bongi or Zanele," no, no, no. They each have to express their opinion, so a meeting that should take fifteen minutes takes two hours. I hear the same suggestions, each time presented as a new concept, voiced over and over again while we gather in a ninety-plus-degree sunbaked field, meeting alfresco. The end result of the meeting is to schedule another meeting. Zulus value relationships over any other human condition, including efficiency, productivity, obligations, or getting what they want. I never really know what most Zulus think because they don't want to disagree with each other and possibly damage a relationship. Relationships are perceived as the key to survival in this collective culture, for better or worse.

Tribal life evolved as a means of protection, of safety in numbers. Your fellow tribal members will pull you up if you fall below a survival level of existence, feed you if you are hungry, and care for you if you are ill. Your very life depends on your tribal family. Maintaining good relationships, at least on the surface, is vital for an individual's survival as well as for the survival of the tribe. But, if you raise yourself up above the level of the tribe, you will be pulled down. The integrity of the tribe requires that all members stay together. Making progress in this environment takes a lot of time.

The Zulu language contains expressions for the jealousy and community rejection that occurs when one member of the tribe becomes noticeably more successful than her peers. A person can be ostracized, or even robbed, if she becomes too successful. Some of the women we train are constrained from developing entrepreneurial endeavors by this fear of rejection.

I find inner peace and unload a backpack full of frustration when I release my need to keep "on schedule." Each day creates itself, and at the end of a day I stir any events or insights into the informational stew I am assembling. I have goals to accomplish, but their definition shifts as I interact with the community. I create a plan then observe whether life and events support my objectives. If not, I evaluate the situation and adjust my plan using new data. It sounds highly intellectual and a bit stuffy, but to boil it down to worn-out buzzwords, I "go with the flow." I assume that what's happening is necessary information to be incorporated into my longer-term plans.

For example, one morning I decide to find iNkosi to ask why there is such limited participation in one entrepreneurial start-up training program. We are trying to empower the women. They need to participate. As I am ready to leave the house, there is a knock on my door. I am annoyed that I will be delayed by this intrusion. iNkosi will leave for a meeting soon and I could miss him. Khati, my young friend, is at the door.

"*Saubona*, Carol. You know Zanele, friend of my mother— she works at the center. In big trouble. Husband home, very drunk, says he will kill her. Please, Missus, drive Zanele to brother in Nqutu."

"Can't anyone help her? Why haven't you called the police?"

"No, Missus, afraid. Must drive her—secret. Please."

With all these prying eyes how can anything be secret? Oh Christ! I didn't sign up for this, but I can't say no.

"Okay."

"Thank you, Carol. Please take *bakkie* to door of visitors center. I bring Zanele."

Khati leaves to get Zanele. I grab the keys to the *bakkie*, drive across the street to the visitors center, and nervously wait in my vehicle, eyes darting around, watching in anticipation that some-one might jump out and attack me. Zanele, clutching a large, slightly torn brown paper bag, slips into the passenger's seat, pulls a scarf over her head, and nods at me to drive off. We clear the

Time, Patience, and Surrender 91

area; she pulls the scarf off her head and opens the bag. In it sleeps a beautiful baby, her two-month-old son. I ask about her three older children. She says her husband will not hurt them. The oldest is twelve and able to care for the nine- and six-year-old. I cringe to think of the domestic possibilities, but for now this is all I can do. Zanele directs me to her brother's house. I drop her off and find my way back to the village.

For days, I survey the environment, watching for a man wanting to punish me for helping Zanele escape. I want to know what happened with Zanele's family, but I am afraid to ask for fear it will expose my role. I trust Beatrice and suspect she knows what happened. I allude to the event. Beatrice responds immediately—she was only waiting for me to ask. Zanele's husband has done this before, even hurt Zanele, but he has left the area to return to work in the city. I ask why the husband abuses Zanele. Beatrice says most men don't like their wives to work, it makes the men feel inadequate as support for the family.

Few men send money to the families they leave behind. What are the women to do? Zanele works in the visitors center and she participates in our training programs. In this place where women are frequently left on their own to make their way alone, in this place that is so bound by the needs of the collective, why do tribal members allow domestic violence? I ask Beatrice if it is customary for the tribe to allow domestic violence. Beatrice says it is not the tribe's business. Zanele could divorce him.

So many things go against my ideas of right and wrong. I could rail against the injustice, fret about my inability to change it, or alternatively try ineffectively to alter that which I am ill equipped to change, draining my energy and wasting resources. It takes greater strength and courage to stay on task, accepting the limitations, and push forward with the projects I can accomplish to uplift their lives.

Events unceasingly conspire to force me to refine my practice of patience. My ability to be patient expands geometrically, but no matter how patient I become, situations demand more. Getting through my days without, at some point, running out of patience and getting annoyed is difficult. I have to find a way to adapt. Perhaps I can transcend the need for patience and learn surrender. Metaphysical and spiritual writings on this concept abound. Surrender doesn't mean giving up. It is a divine detachment, taking whatever comes without reaction, with pure acceptance, in recognition that there is indeed a divine plan at work. The word *patience* implies calmly enduring. In surrender, one has nothing to endure because what happens is part of the plan. If a different outcome is desired, you make another choice, then accept without judgment that which is.

I am determined to learn surrender. Pairing *determined* with *surrender* may be an oxymoron, but my intention is right. First I try to accept with equanimity the small stuff, like the night crawlers as big around as my thumb and twelve inches long that wriggle under the door and squirm around my kitchen after a rain. Or rain leaking in around the windows and causing a muddy mess on the chronically dust-covered floor. Or dropping the empty diesel can on my foot when a scorpion runs across my knuckles. Or coming back from a trip to Durban to find my water tank empty and the pump broken so that I must wash, cook, drink, and flush out of a three-gallon bucket. Or rats crawling on my roof at night, dropping rat poop onto my windowsills. That's life. Surrender.

I surrender to phones that go dead in the middle of a conversation and don't come back on for days. I surrender to airmail that doesn't come for two months. I surrender to an auto insurance company that refuses to take cash or a check or credit card, only a direct withdrawal out of a South African saving account that has been open for more than six months. I accept it all. Life becomes so much more peaceful.

I soon discover that these events are merely undergraduate-level exercises in surrender. A postgraduate course is just around the corner.

It is a Friday morning in October of 2000. iNkosi comes to my cottage to ask me if I am available on Sunday. Yes, I have no plans. Would I be willing to drive some people to St. Augustine's Church for a special (meaning four-hour-long) church service? I am glad to help, that is in part what my *bakkie* is for, community service. My plan: I will drive my passengers to the church and return for them later.

iNkosi tells me that Beatrice is organizing the transport. She requests that I drive my neighbors, the nuns, from the mission convent. Since my *bakkie* is filled with mud—it has been raining and there is mud everywhere—I begin the chore of cleaning it out. The nuns will have to ride in the back as it is a two-door and in theory only holds two passengers. I find some cushions so that the thirty-mile ride to the church won't be too uncomfortable.

At 8:00 Sunday morning, I meet Beatrice in the parking lot near the village church. About twenty people are gathered organizing rides. Beatrice informs me that the service is very special. The bishop has come to confirm new members into the Anglican Church, and our iNkosi will be one. I quickly return to my house and prepare a card of congratulations for him. The nuns gather and politely remove their shoes before climbing into the back of the *bakkie*. What the nuns lack in material wealth they make up for with caloric abundance. Most would tip the scales at close to 200 pounds. To my amazement, they all fit.

Beatrice and Miss Dlamini, both substantial women in their own right, climb into the front seat. I peer tentatively at the *bakkie* before getting in. It lists disturbingly to one side, barely clearing the ground. I take the driver's seat and I look for the gearshift. It is buried under Beatrice's abundant thigh. Beatrice adjusts her position; I extricate the gearshift and proceed to get the truck in reverse. The *bakkie* groans and starts to move ever so slowly. This is going to be a long, slow trip. Even with the most judicious repositioning by Beatrice, I have lost the ability to shift into second or fourth gear, the positions being confiscated by her ample thighs.

As I proceed down the rutted dirt road, passengers sardined in the back, I drive ever so carefully to avoid causing harm to my payload or breaking a strut. At the turnoff to the church, Miss Dlamini informs me that the road is washed out. I have to take the long way around, adding another half hour to the journey. The *bakkie* screams when I try to drive it in first, and then bogs down and chugs like an old jalopy when I shift directly into third. The ladies question the mechanical health of the vehicle. How do I explain that my load would be banned from most U.S. bridge crossings and I am forcing this poor beast of burden to run without benefit of gearing?

We arrive at the church; my plan to return for the nuns is dashed. I must, out of respect for our iNkosi, stay for his confirmation. Already exhausted in anticipation of the four-hour church service ahead, all in Zulu, I roll out of the *bakkie* and, just to amuse myself, watch the nuns unload. One, two, three ... ten women with quiet dignity crawl out of the back of this compact little truck. Zulus, who defy the laws of time, have also mastered defying the laws of space.

Parishioners wait in line to enter the church. Beatrice grabs my hand, cuts through the line, and leads me inside. The service is already in progress. We are directed to the sides of the church, which have been fitted with benches. I sit on the hard wooden plank with Beatrice and the nuns. Its no wonder the nuns are so well padded; they must endure these seats. The main sanctuary of this remarkably beautiful old fieldstone church holds more than 500 and the spacious sides are filled to capacity, about 1,000 people in total. I look around and thank God that the church is made of stone. If it were wood and a fire broke out, the loss of life would be sufficient to make international news.

I notice rows of women sitting together dressed in white, their heads fully covered with long white veils. Across the aisle sit men dressed in their best clothes, all to be confirmed, about 200 in total. An additional 200 people remain outside. The bishop, dressed in ceremonial finery, conducts the service. I look at my watch: 9:30. I set my internal clock to 1:00 P.M., the anticipated end of the service, and prepare in a surrendered state to enjoy it, with no other reasonable choice. Let me point out that I am, once again, the *only* white person in the church. After many months of adapting to only black faces, I forget how unusual I must appear to them. I am quickly reminded when young children stare at me and then giggle and look away with embarrassment when I acknowledge them.

Prayers are prayed, sermons spoken, hymns sung, in a seamless and a seemingly endless cycle. I remember my lesson on the rock. I watch the light as it filters through the high, arched windows and tracks slowly across the floor, marking time in a timeless way. I awaken from my dazed state when the parishioners launch into an exuberant gospel song. I sing "What a Friend I Have in Jesus" in Zulu while old Zulu grannies clap and dance, shouting praise to the Lord. Makes my heart glad to be alive.

I watch children, two to four years old, stand in front of their mothers who are seated in the pews. They remain standing throughout the whole service. The children are so well behaved it astounds me. I once asked how the Zulus get their children to behave so stoically. I was told that the children are well loved but taught expected behavior with scary stories of what happens to children who misbehave. I don't know what it does to their psyches when they are older, but they are certainly obedient when they are young. Children five to ten years old wait outside the church.

By 12:30 I have exhausted all of my tricks to pass time. I move quickly through my reserve of surrender. My store of patience is spent. Thank you, God, only a half hour to go. I can make it. At 12:55 things don't seem to be wrapping up. I lean over to Beatrice and ask what is going on. I hear her say "time for Communion." I must have misunderstood. Each of the 200 confirmees has already taken Communion, *one at a time*. What could Beatrice mean? In about thirty seconds, I find out. Now it is time for the *whole* church congregation to receive Communion. "How can this be?" I say to Beatrice, "There are 1,000 people here." "Yes," she says, "Isn't it wonderful? What a blessing today is."

Patience is long gone and surrender is a forgotten concept. I feel imprisoned, trapped. I start to hyperventilate. I feel like a caged animal. Get me out of here or I will die—or at least scream or maybe throw myself on the mercy of the bishop. I must explain to him I am white, and white people can't do this sort of thing, we aren't made for it. Please, oh please, set me free! Suddenly I feel a wave of divine light wash over me. I know what I must do: flatline my brain waves, go into a numbed state of consciousness. I can, I will, I must make it. I must get through this for the glory of white people everywhere. I sit down and prepare myself. Surrender. Dig deep. I can do it, I can do it.

Slowly each row gets up and proceeds to the front. I use yogic breathing techniques. I am fine. It is our row's turn. I remain seated. I can think of few things I would rather do less at this moment than take Communion from a cup used by hundreds of potentially infected Zulus. Sister Gugu looks at me, smiling. She believes I don't understand what is happening, so she grabs me by the arm and heads down the aisle. I try to explain. Sister Gugu doesn't speak much English, and I don't speak enough Zulu. Plus, she outweighs me by about 100 pounds. I have a choice: lose my arm or go with her.

I wait in line to receive Communion. I am praying like a fool: please, God, don't let there be some horrible disease for which I have no immunity floating around in the chalice. I see only runny noses and sores and hear only coughing. Oh please, God, help. I hear "Trust." Okay, I think to myself, trust. I will trust. I am two people away from the chalice. The man that just finished walks by me with an open sore on his lip. I try to visualize cleansing white light surrounding the chalice. It's my turn. To avoid drinking the contents, I hold my lips together over the edge of the chalice, but the priest tips the cup until I take a sip. Walking back to my seat, I wonder what diseases have just entered my system. I wrap myself in cleansing white light. In my seat, I again try to flatline my brain waves. Only about 500 people to go. No problem, I had nothing else on my schedule today.

Finally, Communion is finished. Praise the Lord. I look around, but no one is leaving. Beatrice nods toward the door. All of the children who were outside are lined up to receive a blessing from the bishop. This is absurd. Why is it happening? I know: it must be an endurance test. With ten years on Wall Street, I always win endurance tests. I sit back down and watch the beautiful faces of the children solemnly, proudly walking down the aisle. What a joyous sight. It is late afternoon: 200 people have been confirmed, 1,000 have taken Communion, 200 children have been blessed. All in a Zulu Sunday. Time to drive my ladies home.

Epilogue: I wake up Wednesday morning with a sore throat and chills. I have the flu. kwaZulu Natal, in addition to having all big-five game animals, also has all big-five diseases: AIDS, tuberculosis, cholera, malaria, and polio. Under these circumstances, the flu is a gift. After a seven-hour Zulu church service, very little can try my patience ever again.

Chapter 11: On Trail in the Wilderness

A SISTER ORGANIZATION TO THE WILD FOUNDATION, the Wilderness Leadership School (WLS), is based in Durban. Dr. Player and his friend Magqubu Ntombela founded the school as a vehicle to share the life-transforming potential of the African bush. Together they pioneered multiracial experiential education, unprecedented and illegal under apartheid. Dr. Player and Mr. Ntombela took influential people, political leaders, writers, reformers, business executives, and philanthropists into the bush hoping that through direct experience of the power and magic of wilderness, the participants would join them in supporting its preservation. The WLS expanded to offer the experience to people of all ages and backgrounds. While living in South Africa I have the experience of a lifetime: being "on trail" with the Wilderness Leadership School.

We stand at the boundary of the Umfolozi Wilderness, one of the oldest game reserves in Africa, anxious to begin our five-day trail experience. No fences separate us from the creatures that inhabit this place. No paths exist to show us the way. Beyond this boundary live lion, rhino, elephant, leopard, hippo, giraffe, zebra, buffalo, hyena, jackal, baboon, warthog, crocodile, antelope, and more. We enter their domain not as predator but as prey.

The school's goal is to have us experience the natural environment in as pure a form as possible. Each participant carries a mat, a sleeping bag, a few items of clothing, and a share of the cooking utensils and food for the group. I've heard many stories about being on trail in the Umfolozi. One group of campers was surprised by a herd of elephants charging through their campsite pursued by a pride of lions. No one was injured. One trail leader, attempting to turn a charging rhino, was gored through the thigh and thrown thirty feet. The campers were unharmed. Eight years ago, our lead guide was camping alone in the wilderness and received a potentially fatal bite from a Mozambique spitting cobra. It was too dangerous to leave in the dark, so he remained in the bush until daybreak, then walked out to find help. Despite these disconcerting tales, thousands of participants have been on trail without one injury. Even so, I am a little apprehensive.

We are seven campers, three men and four women, ages twenty to fifty-plus: a university student, two homemakers, a businessman, a surgeon, a nurse, and me. I'm not sure what I am: a runway from a comfortable life, an adventurer, a humanitarian, an idiot? The two trail leaders, Paul and Michael, tell us to leave watches, books, and extra food behind in the van; they want us to walk in with as little as possible from the outside world. While we reorganize, Paul and Michael inspect their rifles and pack bullets resembling small missiles. Paul announces it's time for our first safety lecture. I'm all ears.

He tells us that the bush we are entering is rather dense, so it is possible for us to surprise a rhino, a buffalo, or even an elephant. If an animal feels surprised or threatened, it could behave in "unreasonable" ways. Personally, I have no desire to reason with a rhino, whatever it wants is okay with me. Paul offers a few suggestions:

"When we encounter animals, do exactly as Michael and I tell you, your lives depend on it." No problem there, glad to oblige.

"Make sure you do not use the chest clip on your backpacks. If we give a command to drop and climb, drop your backpack immediately, no time for two clasps, and climb the closest tree. Climb as far up as you can because rhino are much larger than you might suspect."

He tells a story of a group of campers treed by a rhino. They didn't climb quite far enough and the annoyed rhino managed to dislodge one of the arboreal refugees. Why didn't I learn to climb trees as a kid? Even if we do climb high enough, rhino can push over trees to eradicate annoying little pests, which would, under the circumstances, be us. It is highly unlikely that anything like that will happen, but we should be aware. Next, a quick lesson in Animal Psych 101:

"White rhino are less aggressive than black rhino, but once they decide to charge it is hard to turn them with a warning shot. A white rhino cow will always follow her calf. If a silly little calf charges toward us, mama will follow. Black rhino, on the other hand, might charge more readily but once charging, a warning shot is apt to turn them." Nice to know.

"If we give a signal to be quiet and still, don't move, don't even blink." Thankfully I learned to meditate and can hold quite still.

"Animal behavior is not predicable; much depends on the situation. A lone bull will act very differently from a family group or a mother alone or with her calf. It is the school's policy to protect all inhabitants of the wilderness, human and animal, but if warning shots fail to turn an aggressive animal, we will shoot to kill. We don't want these rare and magnificent beasts harmed. Let's all pay attention and have a safe and wonderful time." Pay attention. I won't let him out of my sight.

We heave our backpacks and head in. Rhino live in thick, thorn-filled brush. Thankfully, I have on long pants instead of shorts. Hiking in the Rocky Mountains taught me that exposed legs get scratched. An hour into our hike, my compatriots' legs look like the aftermath of an angry cat attack. We find animal tracks that our guides call spoor. In hushed tones—Paul doesn't want to scare away any animals—he shows us the different types of spoor: elephant, rhino, hyena, and buffalo. I look around. Thorny acacia trees, strange-looking animal droppings, unusual plants, and oversized animal footprints are constant reminders that we are in Africa. Surrounded by the bush I dissolve into a world of fantasy: I am a great white hunter, or I am Sheena, queen of the jungle, swinging through the jungle canopy on vines.

We walk a few yards more. A white rhino and her calf stand about 100 feet away, calmly browsing. Quietly, we observe the pair. They appear ancient and otherworldly. This isn't *Jurassic Park*: they live here. I lock eyes with the calf, telepathically imploring: stay there. Climbing a thorn tree is not on my wish list of experiences. We walk on, the reality of our cohabitants fixed in my psyche. The guides teach us how to identify different types of wood. Some woods are higher in resins or oils and burn with a hot coal, great for cooking. Thombothi wood makes an excellent fire, especially when wet, but the ash is toxic. Eating food contaminated with the ash can result in intestinal problems. We need to get the wood right.

Our intended camp is on the other side of the White Umfolozi River. The guides warn us that the river is full of crocodiles so we need to cross quickly. In his book *Men, Rivers and Canoes*, Dr. Player describes how each year people are eaten by crocodiles. Crocs can weigh more than 2,000 pounds and are incredibly fast. They have snatched people from riverbanks, pulling them into the water, rolling them over to drown them, and then stuffing the corpse under a submerged ledge to allow it to decompose—a culinary technique that assures a tender and juicy meal. What exactly did the guides mean by cross quickly? I'm thinking a helicopter flyover or at least a boat. As an alternative, this side of the river looks great too! It is winter in the Southern Hemisphere; Michael says the "cold" water makes the crocodiles more sluggish than in the warmer summer months. Very comforting.

Paul shows us how to locate the shallow part of the river. Antelope and buffalo always cross at the shallowest part. We wait in the thicket and watch for animals to cross. Shortly, a small group of impala springs across the river. Paul instructs us to walk to the place where the impala crossed and wait by the riverbank. Paul and Michael load their guns. Paul, gun at the ready, enters the river and crosses, twisting and turning, eyeing the water as he goes. Michael, eyes peeled, covers Paul from the shore. We watch in stunned silence. Once on the other side, Paul walks back, stopping mid-river, and signals to us to cross. Boots off, not a word between us, our eyes betray our unspoken fear. We descend the bank. On the first step, my foot sinks into thick, tenacious mire.

Foot trapped, on my next step I fall to my knees, backpack falling forward and pushing me down. I raise one arm to hold my boots out of the water, the other arm supports my torso. I can't get up. I feel helpless and foolish. I should have released my foot before taking my next step. Michael descends the bank and pulls me to my feet. I am the last to reach the far shore. We sit on the ground about twenty feet from the water's edge wiping sand off our feet, pulling on socks and hiking boots. Michael points to a crocodile 300 feet downstream from our entry point, sliding into the river. I could have been eaten by a crocodile. I can say, without question, that before this day the thought had never entered my brain.

We walk toward our campsite, a rocky, flat area six feet above the river backed by a rock face. This site, only accessible from the riverfront, is safer than an open area where animals can approach from all sides. As we near the site, I hear loud, raucous, and totally unfamiliar sounds. Paul says it is a baboon colony. The males, called dogs, have enormous canine teeth capable of killing humans. "Select a site for your sleeping bags. Once the baboons know where our territory will be, they will calm down." We gather wood and Paul starts a fire to prepare tea. He builds a bush fire: only three sticks of wood arranged in a triangle to create a small flame. Michael collects water from the river. While we wait for the water to boil, Paul conducts his second Welcome to the Wilderness chat.

Topic one: Pooping in the Wilderness

"First, only poop in the daytime. Nocturnal animals are particularly fond of pouncing on prey in compromised positions. You are a squatting duck for lion and leopard, but if it is an emergency and you *have* to poop at night, wake me and I will stand guard with a loaded gun."

I'm thinking I might not poop for the whole trip—better safe than sorry.

Topic two: Toilet Paper

"Toilet paper is not part of an authentic nature experience, we use leaves."

 I can understand how men might think it's no big deal to live without toilet paper, but it's quite a bit different for women. Be reasonable, Paul.

"No dice. No toilet paper. We are one with nature."

He walks a few feet out of camp and returns with leaves. "Use these leaves, but first examine them carefully to make sure they are not covered in pepper ticks. No reason putting pepper ticks on the finish line. They are going to get there eventually, but you should make them work for it."

Pepper ticks? Pepper ticks are teeny-tiny barely visible baby ticks that exist by the billions in the bush. They get on you from just about everywhere and head straight to the soft, moist, tender parts where they dig in (chomp down is more like it) and itch like a #$%&! I surreptitiously count how many pieces of Kleenex I have and calculate how long it will last. Not long enough.

Topic three: Night Watch

"You have to keep a fire with a flame going all night long. Refugees from Mozambique crossing the Kruger Park into South

Africa get eaten by lions because they don't build a fire."

One camper asks if that little fire is big enough. I'm thinking a major blaze is clearly more prudent.

"A bush fire will do the trick as long as it has a flame. Each person on night watch should, at frequent intervals, move around the camp fanning the beam of this flashlight into the darkness. Movement deters animals from entering camp."

Thank goodness it is a seriously large flashlight.

Paul's Rules to Live by (no pun intended):

"Wake me if you hear a lion or a leopard roar in the not-too-far distance; please don't wait until the sound reverberates in your chest cavity before waking me."

"Wake me if your flashlight reflects off the glowing eyes of an animal that you can't identify."

"Wake me if elephant approach, don't wait to be stepped on."

We divide the night into seven single-person shifts and night watch begins.

The first watch stays up, the rest of us retire to our sleeping bags. I lay awake listening to sounds that are new to my ear, unknown animal noises that I am later told are hyena, leopard, toads. ... The full moon rests on the east horizon. I watch as shadows cast by the fire weave stories around the camp. I try to put words to my emotions: appreciation, trepidation, awe. I must remember where the man who follows my night shift sleeps so I wake the correct person. I locate his spot and drift to sleep. I awake to a quiet tap on my shoulder. It is my turn for watch.

I crawl out of my sleeping bag, thoroughly shake out my boots, and retrieve my tea mug. My predecessor hands me the flashlight. He kept the fire going and has a pot of water boiling for tea. Naughty me: I hid my watch in my pants' pocket. It is 1:00 A.M.; the night is stunningly still. I walk the perimeter of the camp, poking the flashlight into the darkness. Here we are little night beasties. You have a whole lot of space to yourselves, no need to come here. I return to the fire and prepare a cup of tea. I sit and listen. I watch the constellations move overhead, feel the stillness, and take comfort in the light of the full moon. I close my eyes to meditate. No distractions. It is easy to sense the contained energy of the earth below and the expansive energy of the sky above. As above so below. I feel harmony, connection, and peace. God is everywhere. It is so obvious. How could anyone doubt it? I feel very protected, very blessed, and very lucky to be here. Another tour around the camp, another cup of tea, another sit. I walk to the edge of the camp for a pee. I won't venture too far into the darkness. My watch is regrettably over. Time to rouse the next in line and return to my sleeping bag to be awakened by the morning light.

The sun announces day two of life in the wild. Lying in my sleeping bag, I listen to sounds of the bush and sounds of the camp. The morning starts slowly. We sit quietly around the fire. With no warning, Paul springs to his feet, grabs his gun, and lunges toward his pack. Startled, I turn to see a rat dragging off a packet of coffee. Paul, elephant gun aimed at this poor rat, screams, "Take my money, take my woman, but never take my coffee!" He shoves his gun at the rat and, regrettably for the rat, pins it against the rock ledge. Paul forcibly separates the rat from the pilfered coffee packet but shows mercy and releases it to live another day. Despite Paul's avowing the pure wilderness experience, I see he makes exception when it pertains to his morning caffeine.

Breakfast is a revoltingly sweet concoction of chocolate-flavored dry cereal with powdered milk. We have used all of the water we packed in and are now drinking Umfolozi River water. The water has a repulsive green color with unidentifiable chewy bits floating abundantly on the surface; the smell is reminiscent of an outhouse at a fish processing plant. Our leaders don't seem too fussy about making sure it boils before drinking it. I, on the other hand, have just spent six years cleansing my body and feeding it only the freshest and healthiest natural foods. My body is pristinely wholesome and crud-free. I am not going to drink that water until it has come to a full boil, an issue that becomes a point of teasing for the South Africans. Even after boiling, the taste is so unpleasant that I cannot force myself to drink it.

We break camp and head off in search of adventure. To avoid scaring off every animal in a five-mile radius, we hike in relative silence. The terrain varies pleasantly. On a sandy river beach, we watch as Cape buffalo enjoy a morning drink and crocodiles sun themselves. In open grassland, we see herds of zebra and warthog. We cross a floodplain where the grass is so thick that we can't see our feet. Not a comforting feeling. Paul is leading the walk. His hand flashes up to signal "Halt." He places his finger to his mouth for us to be quiet and waves at us to back up quickly. He heard the hiss of a Mozambique spitting cobra. Since almost dying from a bite, he has a healthy respect for getting out of its way. We give the area a wide berth.

At a clearing, we break for lunch: dried fruit, crackers, and cheese. We ask Paul if he is nervous always being the first person in line walking through the bush. He says the third person in line is the one usually bitten by the snake. The first person startles the snake, the second person annoys it, and the third person pays the price. I am the third person. Our walk continues, more beautiful landscape and more animals. Any initial fear I had has dissipated. I belong in this place, not in concrete jungles and high-rise apartments, not in traffic jams and crowded shops. This is real. This feels like home.

Our second campsite is on a cliff overlooking the river. It is late afternoon. We prepare tea to take to the cliff's edge to watch evening events unfold. Cape buffalo and various antelope gather at the river for their evening drink. Three elephants lumber ever so slowly into view. Most American zoo elephants are Asian elephants. They are much smaller and easier to transport than African elephants, which are enormous. Males can weigh 15,000 pounds and stand seventeen feet tall—imagine a two-story bedroom walking toward you. There are lovely old trees along the bend in the riverbank. The elephants wrap their trunks around branches, snapping them off the way I would pick a blade of grass. As each branch breaks it sounds like gunfire cracking in the distance. One bull elephant is particularly enamored with the upper branches of the tree. He stands on his hind legs, straining his back as he wills his trunk to reach the topmost branches. He is stretched so high on his hind legs, trunk extended skyward, that he looks like a giant ballerina from a Disney animation. We expect him to topple over backward, but finally he manages to wrap the tip of his trunk around the chosen branch. With the force of a falling building and the sound of thunder, he drops to the ground, splitting the enormous old tree in two. Seemingly satisfied with his triumph, the elephant proceeds to dine. With delicate movements of his trunk, using his tusks as levers, he methodically selects leaves, skipping some, eating others, slowly progressing along the length of the branch. Darkness interferes with our view, so I reluctantly return to the fire and await supper.

Anything eaten in the great outdoors after a day of hiking is enjoyed far beyond its culinary due. We set upon the macaroni and cheese like starved dogs, using our fingers to remove any trace of foodstuff left on our plates or in the pot. After supper, we fix tea and sit around the fire sharing impressions of the day. As we prepare for bed, dividing the night into shifts and claiming sleeping sites, we hear the roar of a lion. Never believe that man has evolved beyond his primal instincts. The instant the lion roars, my bowels clench and the urge to run—fast—consumes me. A second later, we hear the agonized cry of a beast. Paul says we are listening to lions kill a young Cape buffalo. The camp is silent as the sounds paint a gruesome scene. We listen to the calf's cries as the lions finish the hunt and then we hear the triumphant moans of victory as they eat their evening meal. Quietly, reflectively, we proceed to bed, armed only with a flashlight for night watch.

The sounds of the night disturb my innocence. For me life has never involved a struggle to survive. I hear lions, leopard, and hyena performing their roles, bequeathing death, sustaining life. The reality of how exposed I am is ever so much clearer. I feel insignificant pitted against the biological imperative to live. Night watch is solemn and tense, but also expansive, exploring new emotions and a new way of being in relation to nature.

I awake with pepper ticks thirstily enjoying the blood brought closer to the skin's surface by the pressure of the elastic band on the bottom edge of my bra. Lions may have the right to feed on a Cape buffalo calf, but these creations of Satan have no right to dine on me. I borrow a compatriot's concoction of essential oils and rub it onto the area. The lotion is purported to repel the vermin and relieve the itch. I consult my female companions who confess to the same insect foul play. We decide to eliminate the feedlot and store our bras for the duration.

Over our morning cuppa and a vanilla-flavored version of the same toxically sweet cereal, aching shoulders surface as a universal complaint. We ask our guides if we may camp a second night in the same spot, allowing us to hike without our packs. We take our plates and pot from last night's dinner down to the river for a cleaning. Soap is not in our guides' vocabulary. Not authentic. They suggest we use the shallow six-inch-deep part of the river and scrub ourselves and the dishes with sand. The guides warn us to avoid the deeper part of the river; crocodiles may be lurking. I give myself a sniff. Not too bad. Certainly not bad enough to justify scrubbing with sand in a crocodile-infested river.

We hang by the river watching animals on the far shore, organize ourselves, and head inland for day three of *Wild Kingdom*. The guides lead us to an area heavily used by rhino. White rhino males mark their territory by pooping in the same place, breaking the poop up, and scattering it in an area called a midden. It is about the size of a wading pool. Paul marches us right into poop pit, picks up a handful of dried poop, and rolls it around in his hand, picking through the bits and sniffing it. He declares that all of the mysteries of rhino life can be discerned in a handful of poop. He hands me a yummy great glob, proudly instructing me on how one can tell white rhino poop from black rhino poop. Not sure I want to know, but as long as I'm here. ... My inner-child fantasy surfaces. I am a great bush scientist ruggedly uncovering the mysteries of the wilderness armed only with my senses and a native as a guide. We continue our trek, more animals, more poop, more mysteries uncovered.

On Trail in the Wilderness   113

Back at camp, my head is aching. Two months into my stay in South Africa I was initiated into life in the bush with a case of tick bite fever. Tick bite fever is like Lyme disease but usually doesn't have the same serious aftereffects. Its victim just feels like death for a week or more, enduring chills, aches, and splitting headaches. I am concerned that my tick bite fever headaches have returned. I also suspect that I may be dehydrated. Every time I take a swallow of water my stomach rebels. Both the taste and the smell revolt me. Boiling neither eliminates the smell nor improves the taste. Chlorine tablets make it worse. Instead of tasting like an outhouse at a fish processing plant, it tastes like a latrine near a locker room at a public pool.

I fanaticize about a large bottle of refreshing, thirst-quenching Rocky Mountain springwater. Alas, I have to make peace with this swill. I'm feeling none too rugged at the moment so I take a little nap and wake in time for dinner. Dinner is a curry of freeze-dried veggies and tofu. I'm in heaven—well almost. Paul made the curry with enough chili to strip the lining off my intestinal tract. I choke down some cooled tea.

After dinner, Paul gives us lessons on the night sky: we see the Southern Cross, the constellation Scorpio, and the Milky Way. As I prepare for bed, I think about how I am going to tell family and friends about this experience. I hope that the power and magic aren't lost in the telling.

Day four arrives. My sleeping bag and pack are wet, not from rain but from very heavy dew. Paul cautions that we should prepare for rain; a weather front is approaching. All of our clothes and sleeping bags must be packed in plastic. The possibility of rain is surprising; winter is the dry season. After preparing our belongings for wet weather, we walk to the beach to observe the morning rituals at the river. A lone elderly bull Cape buffalo suns himself on the sand. When male Cape buffaloes become too old to oversee a herd of females, a younger bull replaces them and the old males leave the herd to live their remaining years in solitude. The rules of nature are forever practical, without a whiff of sentimentality.

Our group is quiet this morning. Perhaps after three days of intense exposure to our evolutionary roots we are in a reflective place. Without comment, Paul stands and begins a slow walk downriver. Emerging from the bush into a clearing, we surprise a large group of white rhino cows, young bulls, and calves. They sense us and become agitated. The cows regroup, forming a protective line in front of the younger animals. The guides motion us to huddle up (so we look bigger), stand still, and be quiet. Nobody breathes. The rhino are about 300 feet away. Paul whispers, "Don't look directly at them, it signals a challenge." We're supposed to pretend we are la-di-da-ing our way through the bush and don't notice the rhino! Get real—they are four-legged Humvees with bad eyesight and worse tempers. I fear the rhinos will hear my heart pounding, think it's native drumming, take it as a threat, and charge. We are in a tight standoff, neither side moving. Paul and Michael load their rifles and place a second bullet between their teeth. The younger male rhino move into formation. We stand in ossified silence. Time evaporates. Has it been thirty seconds or thirty minutes? Finally the lead rhino slowly turns away, dissipating the tension. We back up and exit the clearing.

We have walked only a short distance when it starts to rain. Fortunately, I have a great waterproof rain outfit that I whip out and whip on in a flash. The rest of the troop dons whatever rain gear they have. Two South Africans have South African army surplus raincoats. Within minutes they are soaked to the skin. The South African army must be too tough to mind a little rain.

The guides leave to find a site to set up rain flies, paper-thin sheets of nylon to protect us from the rain. We will wait here. The temperature drops and the rain increases; things are getting quite unpleasant. Lunch, anybody? We huddle together to protect our food from getting wet, but rain drips off our noses. The crackers are soggy before we get them to our mouths.

I worry about hypothermia for the others. I am cold, but at least I'm dry. Others aren't. Two of our group are turning an alarming shade of blue. We try to keep up our spirits and stay warm as the pelting rain continues. We laugh through jumping jacks and hopping games. The guides return. They set up three rain flies that are very delicate, but if we don't touch them and split up into three groups we can be dry in a few minutes. The flies are tied between bushes about three feet off the ground. We crawl under and wriggle out of our wet clothes then wrap up in our sleeping bags. The rain stops in about an hour. I redress in my damp clothes.

Paul tells us to collect thombothi wood, as it will burn when wet. We return with enough thombothi wood to create a sizable conflagration. Both guides criticize our excessive behavior. At that point, I am so cold and uncomfortable that I could set fire to the whole darn forest. A touchy-feely, environmentally conscious sensibility can be short-lived when one is cold, tired, hungry, and generally miserable. I take note not to be so judgmental of the tribal people who cut down the trees for firewood.

We will cook over thombothi wood this evening, but not to worry, the ash won't kill us. Consistent with its reputation, the thombothi wood catches fire. My headache returns. I must be dehydrated. I wait by the fire for the water to boil, but the fire is so weak it doesn't generate sufficient heat. I absolutely will not drink unboiled water. My headache gets worse. I pass on supper and go to bed. As I undress, my odor wafts upward. How in the world am I going to reenter society smelling like this? For that matter, how am I going to get through the night smelling myself? Miscellaneous bites and pepper ticks cover my body. Too tired to care, I fall asleep, survive night watch, return to bed, and awake groggy and out of sorts.

Day five, the last day. It is damp, gray, and cool, but there is no more rain. My headache pounds on. Rejecting breakfast, I force down some chlorinated water and wait for others to decide what to do before hiking back to the van this afternoon. One person wants to learn more about tracking. Paul says there is a crocodile-free swimming hole in a tributary of the Umfolozi. He will teach us tracking on our way. Maybe I can rinse off some of the grime there.

We walk beside the stream, spot lots of spoor, and have more lessons of the wild. We find two small pools of water out of view of each other. The sky is clear; the sun gently warms us. The men gather at one pool, women at the other. We strip and, as casually as women putting on lipstick in a bathroom mirror, proceed to comb through our pubic hair, under our breasts, and behind our knees to remove unwanted bloodsucking beasties. Five days in the bush and we are comfortably simian. How easy and natural it feels. There is no hint of awkward embarrassment, the restrictions of society are meaningless under the circumstances. We play and splash, laugh, then dress, refreshed and smelling tolerable.

As I walk back to the van and back to my life in the village, I know that this experience changed my sense of self. I spent many weeks in the Rocky Mountain wilderness; this wilderness is vastly different. The difference is not the geography or the unique wildlife. An intangible primal essence emanates from this place that connects all lives. I grasp how relationships in nature are sacred unto themselves and how humans judge behavior and value resources from our own limited perspective, using our fears and needs as benchmarks of right and wrong. In five days I have become more alive but less worldly, more enlightened but with fewer answers, and more at peace but seeking truth.

Chapter 12: iNkosi's Birthday

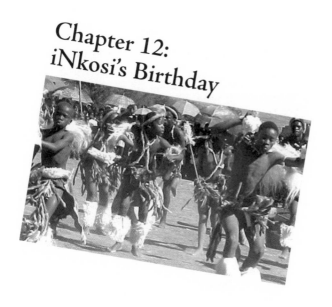

ONE OF THE GREAT PERKS of my job in Zululand is traveling with Vance and Maggie when they come in-country. The travel provides a much-needed break from my 24/7 isolation and affords me a broader perspective in which to view the issues this community faces. During their first visit, Maggie wants to go to the Maputuland Coast of Natal, just south of the Mozambique border. The day after our return is iNkosi's thirty-seventh birthday. To help solidify his position in the tribal area, WILD wants to celebrate his birthday as a special occasion. Before we depart, I help organize the party.

iNkosi is a very thoughtful man, but not quick at making decisions. It is the Zulu way to consider all choices carefully and consult elders and others, no matter how insignificant the decision is by Western standards. Consultation polishes the surface of cordial relationships and offers less opportunity for criticism. A South African warned me never to ask a Zulu to make a decision on the spot. It just doesn't work. Instead, he suggested that I provide a time line for a decision. After weeks of discussion, we finally settle on a large, formal party, meaning the entire tribe will be invited and an ox slaughtered. The party will be held at "town hall," the meeting room at Isandlwana primary school. Before leaving on the trip, I give cash to Miss Dlamini for supplies, confirm plans with iNkosi and Beatrice, and make sure everyone knows I won't be back until the day before the party. I leave confident that all will be ready on my return.

Maggie, Pat, Vance, and I drive to a wilderness lodge on the Maputuland Coast. The lodge is situated in a remote cove inaccessible by road. Staff from the lodge meet us at a designated rendezvous site. We transfer to a four-wheel-drive dune buggy for a thirty-minute trip through spectacular forested sand dunes. Our rooms are tastefully appointed tree houses. The dining area, bar, and lounge are all outdoors.

A tame bush baby lives on-site. Bush babies look like a cross between a squirrel and a koala bear. They are incredibly cute, with the sweetest faces I have ever seen. Their call belies their appearance. They create a hideous racket for such endearing little things. Each night the tame bush baby arrives at the bar, crawls around drinks and over snack bowls, making its way to the bartender. The bartender gives the bush baby a banana, which it eats on the spot. Unable to resist the urge, I pet the bush baby as it sits on the bar. The bartender warns me, "It can bite. You should leave it. The thing is a pest. One night I ran out of bananas. The little brat threw a wobbly, knocking glasses and bowls off the bar. I'd like to get rid of it."

The area is overrun with vervet monkeys. Male vervets, also called blue-balled monkeys, have unique anatomy. Their testicles are disproportionately large and bright blue, and they have cherry red penises. When they want to impress or threaten, they puff up their genitals and swagger around upright with their pelvises jutting forward, a not-to-be-missed exhibition, but a behavior I am grateful human males do not mimic, at least not precisely. The monkeys seem quite comfortable around humans and play freely along the forest paths.

I drape a wet shirt over the railing of my tree house. As soon as I turn my back, a monkey takes off with it. The monkey carries the shirt to the upper branches of the tree far out of my reach. "Bring it back you little thief!" I shout. The troupe dances in the trees near the shirt, taunting me. The next morning, after a delightfully noisy night listening to the sounds of the forest, I find my shirt, well soiled and slightly torn, abandoned in a heap on the thatch roof with thatch strewn all over the front deck of my room. What destructive little pests, but cute!

I stroll through the magnificent, lush forest and along the pristine beach. I am thankful that it is winter—not too hot and few mosquitoes. In the summer months this is a high malarial area, and I am not enthusiastic about taking any of the antimalarial drugs. I have heard almost as many horrifying stories about complications from antimalarial drug use as issues with the disease. Westerners have little idea how serious a threat malaria still is.

As a little girl, I deep-sea fished with my uncle off the Florida coast, but I have never fished from a beach into the surf. The lodge supplies fishing gear. Vance is anxious to fish and convinces me to join him. He catches a beautiful little pompano and asks me to hold the fish while he removes the hook. The fish makes croaking noises as it trembles in my hand, struggling for life. I urge Vance to hurry as I apologize to the fish for catching it and gently returned it to the sea. Vance finds this behavior quite amusing and teases me for days. That is the beginning and the end of my career as a catch-and-release fisherman. I heartily endorse sustainable fishing for food, but terrifying and potentially harming fish for pleasure doesn't seem equitable.

Our trip to Maputuland is a beautiful and relaxing respite from my confining life in the village. We return to Isandlwana on Thursday evening. Maggie, Vance, and I are tightly scheduled in meetings with regional politicians and businessmen on Friday, the day before iNkosi's birthday party. As soon as I walk in the door of my home, Beatrice hustles across the street. She must have been watching for my return.

"We need your help for the party. iNkosi is most concerned. Nothing has been done and he is afraid he is to be embarrassed."

"What do you mean nothing has been done?"

"Invitations have not been given out, the primary school has a soccer rally in the meeting room, and we have no food. We need a place for the honored guests and dignitaries to have lunch. Will you host a lunch here in your house?"

"Why has nothing been done? I gave Miss Dlamini money and you and iNkosi agreed on the plan."

"We thought is best to wait for you."

My gut reaction was to yell, "What the hell did you do before I got here?" but reason and constraint rule. One word explodes in my head: *surrender*. I walk to the lodge and inform Vance of the condition of iNkosi's birthday party. Fortunately, Vance is a master problem solver. I am too frustrated to concentrate on creating solutions. He organizes a plan to have Miss Dlamini driven to the grocery store tomorrow morning and locates plates and cups for tribal guests. At his request, Pat graciously agrees to host the luncheon for the dignitaries. He asks Miss Dlamini to inform the school principal that it is vital for us to use the school meeting hall so they must move the soccer rally. Now all we have to do is to find a master of ceremonies and set a program for the party. I return to my house for a fitful night's sleep. Early Friday morning, people begin stopping by my house to ask me what program plans I have made for iNkosi's party. Why is it my job? What do I know about preparing for tribal celebrations? Can't anyone be proactive?

Miss Dlamini returns from shopping late Friday afternoon with food for 500. Thank goodness she organized a group of village women to help cook. Vance and I use the *bakkie* to shuttle food, supplies, and people up the hill to Miss Dlamini's *muzi*. On one trip, we arrive just in time to witness the slitting of the throat of the sacrificial ox. I turn away from the sight but I can't avoid the sound. I am in agony listening to its moans as it bleeds to death. I admit I am just one big animal-loving sissy, although Zulu cows are hard to love. They ball up traffic, standing immovably in the road, and leave cow pies everywhere. Their overall demeanor is exceedingly dull-witted. Still, my appetite will be sated with rice and beans, thank you very much. As soon as the ox stops moaning and flailing, the men skin it. The scene around the *muzi* evokes images of long-ago military encampments. Huge, ancient cast-iron pots on legs are set over wood fires. Miss Dlamini's kitchen, a square stone and cement building, contains three ovens, two gas and one wood, with a center worktable and room for helpers. Biscuits bake, chicken stews, coleslaw marinates, and beans soak. We leave hopeful.

Early the next morning I walk to Miss Dlamini's to check on their progress. The women worked through the night and are still hard at it. Food in aluminum bowls, wooden bowls, on baking trays, and in enameled pots is stacked everywhere. I arrive in time to watch the final dismemberment of the cow. A man, one foot planted on what is left of the cow's head, is sawing off the ears. The hide is staked out on the ground, bloody side up, drying.

The rest of the cow simmers in the large iron kettles balanced over wood fires. Good thing I spent time in a hospital pathology lab, it prepared me for the sight. We city dwellers only get as close to animal slaughter as the plastic wrap on a T-bone steak.

Vance arrives and conducts a little reconnaissance while I check in with Miss Dlamini. Joining us, he suggests I look into one of the four large kettles to see what is cooking. "Just go over and lift the lid," he says. Once the steam clears, I am peering into a revolting gray mass of simmering cow parts; the cow's nose, intact, pokes up out of the cauldron, giving the illusion that the cow is submerged in the bubbling glop, holding its nose up to breathe. I replace the lid, pausing for a moment to consider the flavor-enhancing qualities of bovine boogers. Yummy.

In the midst of all the activity, no one knows where iNkosi is or when the birthday boy will arrive for his party. He still lives a distance away with his mother, and they still have no phone. Preparations continue, but the timing remains uncertain. Reverend Zulu from St. Augustine's church arrives. He graciously volunteers to be master of ceremonies. After exerting a little well-placed political pressure, we are permitted to use the primary school meeting room. The soccer rally is moved to a nearby field. We decorate the lodge and the town hall with the crepe paper Miss Dlamini brought back from town, transport food from Miss Dlamini's *muzi* to both locations, and try to organize the attendees. After much hand-wringing, iNkosi arrives late morning. The celebration can now begin.

It is a very joyous, formal, and traditional event. At one end of the town hall, an elevated platform serves as a stage. The rest of the room is filled with simple wooden benches. A primitive mural depicting the Ten Commandments covers the walls. The dignitaries sit on the elevated platform with iNkosi, while the

villagers fill the benches. Each person on the platform is introduced to the assembly. Zulus have a tradition of naming people
after their personalities or physical characteristics. I am named
"the woman without a husband" and am good-heartedly introduced as such. I have certainly been called worse.

Tribal councilmembers, dressed in traditional animal skins
and carrying spears, clubs, and shields, perform an ancient dance
of welcome honoring the iNkosi. The dance is powerful, reverent,
and warlike. The men shout, prance, wave spears, and bow down
to the leader. Village women perform a traditional dance of
honor and then a dance called *toi-toi* that is happy, playful, and
exuberant. Lots more drumming. I love Zulu drumming.

I remember attending a drumming workshop in 1993 at a
retreat in upstate New York. The world-renowned Babatunji
Olatunji, leader of the group Drums of Passion, conducted the
workshop. There were 250 white African-drumming wannabes.
He divided the attendees into groups, each group drumming a
part of the rhythm. Individually it was nothing special, but put
together it was pure magic. I left the auditorium to lie on the
ground outside. The beat of the drums reverberated through my
body. It was powerful, primal, and instinctual. Zulu drumming is
more so.

The children dance next, enthusiastic, extravagant, and playful.
There are speeches, singing, teasing, and laughter. We present
iNkosi with birthday gifts and proceed to lunch. The villagers
remain at the town hall with an army of women to serve the huge
cauldrons of food. Members of the royal family, the tribal council,
and visiting *amakosi* are shuttled to the lodge. For many, it is their
first opportunity to visit the lodge. Some are dressed in traditional
costumes while others are dressed in elaborate clothes merging
Western styles and African fabrics in exotic designs. It is a collage

transcending time, social structure, and perceptions of elegance. Toasts and speeches continue. I am amazed at the plentiful and beautifully presented meal pulled together at the last minute thanks to the tireless efforts of the women of the community and the kitchen staff at the lodge. I collapse, more emotionally spent than physically exhausted. It feels like we organized a military campaign, but it was accomplished with style. iNkosi is honored and everybody is pleased.

Chapter 13: Miss D

A GUIDING PRINCIPLE OF THE WILD FOUNDATION requires leaders be identified early in the program development phase, then be trained and mentored to take over management of the program as quickly as possible. Local empowerment rather than dependence is our goal. iNkosi was the first person selected in the leadership mentoring program. His trip to the States for training at Shenandoah University is part of this process. We are fortunate that the tribal council allowed Miss Elizabeth Dlamini, their tribal secretary for more than twenty years, to accept the position as resident program manager.

Miss D, as I affectionately and respectfully call her, is a remarkable woman. She was born and raised exclusively in the Mangwe-Buthanani tribal area. She graduated from the local high school and took advantage of rural training programs offered by the government. Her education is a product of her own vision, ambition, and tenacity. Of all the locally reared tribal members, she speaks the most fluent English. Her *muzi* houses her many businesses. She is an accomplished sewer, makes beer, bakes bread and cakes, and creates craftwork for sale to support her mother, her three children, and various family members. She conducts classes training fellow tribe members in the skills she has developed. If she believes that her tribal cohorts have been given sufficient training and resources to allow for a hand up and they don't try, she is quick with her criticism. Lazy is lazy, no excuses.

A born feminist, Miss D, despite severe cultural pressure, never married and never spoke to me about the fathers of her children. All she would say when asked about men is that they are "not much use." They just sit around, do nothing, and make more work. From her twenty years as tribal secretary, she knows everybody's business and secrets: who killed whom when, which families have problems with each other, who the crooks are, and who embezzled how much money. She has an amazing recall for dates and numbers. If asked how much money was spent on a project two years ago, she can quote it to the rand. If asked why a particular person is treated with fear-scented deference, she will reply something like, "On 19 March 1991 he had so-and-so killed but bribed the police and got out of the charge."

Under other circumstances, she would have made an extraordinary police investigator. She loves all things having to do with criminal behavior and catching the bad guys. Miss D leverages the situations of her fellow tribal members to solve crimes. Zulu boys, from the time they can walk, are sent into the fields to watch their family's cattle. With little else to do—Zulu cows are uniquely slow moving—the boys watch everything that goes on, creating a network of human surveillance cameras. If anything goes missing, Miss D questions her army of boys and eventually one of them comes forward with the information she desires.

In the first year, our relationship develops slowly. Around me she is soft-spoken, reserved, with head down and eyes averted. She is understandably suspicious of my activities and motivations. Her breadth of knowledge, common sense, wisdom, and skills impress me. She maintains all vital records for the tribe, manages the money, organizes meetings, and follows up on tribal business. She is known as the best Zulu beer maker in the village. If you have not had a chance to try Zulu beer, I don't recommend it. It's made by fermenting corn and sorghum (and occasionally other bits and pieces of leftover vegetable matter) in a clay pot for three to four days, then filtering it through a woven-grass tube. The cloudy liquid has a raw, yeasty taste that must be acquired to be appreciated. The residual corn mash gets fed to the chickens. It's easy to tell which *muzi* just finished making a batch of beer: their chickens have a peculiar wobble to their walk.

In June 2001, The WILD Foundation sponsors Miss D's attendance to a six-week program at Shenandoah University in Virginia, the same program that iNkosi attended during the summer of 1999. She takes classes in English, democracy, business, and computers. Miss D has never lived outside of the area and has never seen a large airplane, much less ridden in one. I can't imagine how far removed from her life experience the trip is going to be. The first event of the journey is a four-hour drive to Durban, a city of more than a million people, to get her visa for entry into the United States.

We drive to Durban the afternoon before our 8:00 A.M. appointment at the U.S. consulate. Safe surroundings, especially in Durban, are a very high priority. Vance is adamant that the safety risk of staying in a low-budget hotel is not worth the few dollars saved. We can get a nice hotel room with a full breakfast for $30 each. I want to treat Miss D to her own room. We check into the hotel before dark. I show Miss D around her room, how the color TV and bath work. She is quiet and attentive. I leave her to enjoy her evening. The next morning we meet at breakfast. When I ask if she slept well, she replies that she fell asleep watching TV. She really liked the hot shower. It might have been the first hot shower in her life, but I don't think it appropriate to ask.

I coordinate a visit to the States with a stopover in England and Miss D's trip to Virginia. I will fly with her from Durban to Johannesburg to familiarize her with the airplane before her seventeen and a half hour flight to the United States. On the morning of our departure, Miss D's family members gather with Beatrice and iNkosi for a prayer send-off. It is a joyous event with warm expressions of delight and goodwill—a wonderful way to celebrate her journey. On our flight, Miss D learns how the airplane seat works, where the toilets are, and about the food service. On the surface, she appears poised and calm, seemingly unflappable. As we maneuver through the Johannesburg airport, she remains quiet, but is wide-eyed. I escort her to the gate for her flight to America before boarding my plane to London. Miss D has a list of phone numbers and instructions on how to call her U.S. contacts if anything goes amiss. An associate of WILD will meet Miss D's plane in Atlanta and help her transfer to her flight to Washington, D.C., I say a little prayer that Miss D will arrive at her final destination without a hitch. Miss D, Vance, and I are scheduled to meet at Shenandoah University at the end of July.

After a delightful activity-intensive social schedule in Boulder, I am ready to return to my quiet, secluded life in Isandlwana, but first I will visit Miss D. Vance and I meet in Washington and travel together to Shenandoah University. Miss D lives on campus in a dormitory with students from Paraguay, Korea, and five other developing countries. We arranged to meet her in the campus cafeteria. She walks in, noticeably thinner, carrying textbooks and spiral notepads. A young dormmate from Korea persuaded Miss D to exercise with her in the campus gym. A 190-pound Zulu matron on a stationary bike in a campus gym? The image short-circuits my brain. You can't get much farther away from her life in Zululand than that! Miss D says she enjoys her classes and her fellow students very much. Her English scores are improving, she loves the business course, but confides that the computer is difficult to learn. We arrange for tutoring assistance on the computer. She must know how to use e-mail and the word processing program so we can communicate after I return to the States.

During the time I have known Miss D, through myriad new experiences, I have never seen such a look of delight or heard more enthusiasm in her voice than when talking about visiting the Lincoln and Jefferson Memorials and the Washington Monument. She says she never imagined buildings so beautiful existed. These monuments were built for people like you, Elizabeth, to remind us that it is every human's right to be equal and free.

Miss D completes her classes in good order. A veteran of transatlantic travel, she manages the plane change in Johannesburg by herself. Beatrice and I meet her at the Durban airport. She walks out through customs, twenty pounds thinner, wearing a blue-and-white striped seersucker business suit and carrying a notebook computer over her shoulder and a book bag over her arm. Time travel does exist. In two months, Miss D traveled two centuries forward in time. Her experiences could change the destiny of the women of the Mangwe-Buthanani tribe.

From the time WILD officially hired Miss D in early 2001 until her return from the United States in August 2001, she continued to hold her position as tribal secretary. This overlap allows the tribal council to locate, hire, and train a new tribal secretary and lets Miss D get comfortable working for WILD before committing to the position. Her dual role benefits WILD. She is our eyes and ears in the tribal council meetings and keeps us informed on tribal issues and events. Our relationship evolves nicely. When she talks to me, she meets my gaze and answers questions in detail, even volunteers information and suggestions. She is by far my most reliable and prolific source of information in Isandlwana.

Miss D helps me understand the complex and convoluted arena of Zulu politics. Political party affiliation represents more than just voting history or ideological preferences. The choice can be a life or death decision. The African National Congress (ANC) is the dominant political party in South Africa, so dominant that there is effectively a one-party system. Zulu Prince Buthelesi broke off from the ANC and started his own political party, the Inkhata Freedom Party, or IFP, which became the majority party in kwaZulu-Natal province. Although the balance of power in kwaZulu-Natal has recently shifted in favor of the ANC, many rural Zulus remain members of the IFP.

When I ask people in the village about political party affiliation, my inquiry is always met with nervous glances and vague answers. In my first meeting with iNkosi, he warns me that I must, for my own safety, remain politically neutral. Time to ask Miss D about the political party intrigue. She explains that, when given the right to vote, black South Africans were not introduced to the political party system correctly. They were not taught about the function of political parties in a free society. Instead, local power brokers strongly influenced, in other words threatened, people into joining their political party. Belonging to a political party became the equivalent of belonging to a religion—it was potential reason for extermination. Zulus belonging to the ANC are suspect, travel together, and are considered near treasonous by some. An ANC member walking through an IFP area could be killed, and vice versa.

Miss D has no use for politics or politicians. The greatest insult she can inflict on a person is to accuse them of being a politician. They promise anything, deliver nothing, are crooked, pompous, and basically useless. It's actually not too far from my own understanding of many political systems. The advantage in the United States is that we have blessedly evolved out of making political affiliation a cause for murder—now they're just cause for ridicule, grandstanding, and disagreements.

Miss D amazes me with her grounded, practical, no-nonsense approach to life. She will embrace as fact or discard as foolishness traditional Zulu beliefs, according to her experience. She finds silly the royal family's belief that when a tree planted near a *muzi* grows taller than the headman's house, the headman will die. Her *muzi* has beautiful old jacaranda trees surrounding it. In a conversation with her about weather, I am delightfully surprised when I stumble onto a thought-provoking aspect of traditional Zulu life.

It has rained for a two days. Miss D and I plan to visit two of our community development projects. If the rain stops and the sun comes out for a day, the roads, such as they are, will be passable. If the rain continues, the roads will be rivers of intractable mud for a week. Zulus, like most people living close to the land, understand weather patterns and are fairly effective predictors of rain, so I ask Miss D how much longer the rain will continue. She answers definitively that the rain will stop on Sunday afternoon, three days from now. I ask how she knows it will stop precisely then. I expect an answer involving wind patterns and clouds. Instead, she tells me that a woman will be buried Sunday afternoon and it will rain until then. Why is that? The woman was a *sangoma*, or medicine woman, who could hold off rain for special occasions: weddings, funerals, and the like. I ask how the *sangoma* learned to hold off the rain. She was taught by the previous rain *sangoma*. When that old woman was alive, if tribal members wanted rain, they would get her drunk and then make her mad. When she was mad it would rain cats and dogs—or so I was told. We decide to postpone the visits until the following week. It rained until Sunday afternoon.

Chapter 14:
Crafts, Crops, and Capitalism

ALTHOUGH TEACHING IS MY JOB, learning occupies much of my time. Working with the Zulu women trains me in a valuable skill: knowing the balance between giving people a chance to manage themselves and understanding when it is time to step in and take charge.

A Durban-based nonprofit, EMBO Craft, offers a sewing workshop in the tribal area. EMBO Craft's mission is the economic improvement and the social empowerment of women. They provide hand-crank sewing machines for each trainee. The operator's left hand guides the material under the needle while the right hand rotates a small wheel on the side on the machine. Twenty women are taught how to make items from scraps of fabric donated to EMBO Craft from clothing and upholstery manufacturers. They sew patchwork vests, placemats, tote bags, tea cozies, and pillow covers. Each participant is obliged to train five more women. Once accomplished, the sewing machine is theirs to keep. By the end of the program, 100 women have been trained.

The patchwork is wonderfully colorful, unusual, and functional—ideal for the tourist trade. But not one person produces any goods for sale.

Wanting to build on that training, Miss D and I decide to launch a combination sewing club and small business start-up. I contact EMBO Craft for advice on how to persuade the women to sew items for sale. The EMBO Craft trainer suggests that a second workshop might produce sufficient confidence in the women's newly acquired skills for them to move forward with production. EMBO Craft has recently launched an innovative program that built on the skills they taught in the previous workshop. The new weeklong workshop combines teaching craft skills such as fabric dyeing, fabric painting, and embroidery with basic business skills training. An AIDS awareness program is deftly woven into the workshop. The goal of the AIDS awareness segment is simple: have the workshop participants acknowledge that AIDS exists. When prevention is the only cure, acknowledging that the disease exists is vital to stop its spread. Undiagnosed, the AIDS epidemic goes unacknowledged. If asked, the villagers say people die from a headache, stomach problems, or a bad chest—no one dies of AIDS.

St. Vincent's church was the official host of the September 1999 workshop. The trainers stayed with Beatrice for three days. I hope Beatrice will again allow the trainers to stay with her. When I receive the detailed curriculum for the new EMBO Craft workshop, I explain it to Beatrice. I describe the craft skills training, the business skills training, and the AIDS awareness work. Beatrice asks if I would please tell EMBO Craft to remove the section on AIDS.

"The women do not like to talk about it. They are not comfortable."

"Beatrice, do you know that hundreds of thousands of Zulus are dying from AIDS? Before the disease is finished, millions of Zulus will die. Once a person gets HIV/AIDS, they die from it. There is no cure. Black or white, rich or poor, American or South African, AIDS kills everyone who gets it. If we can't talk about it we can't stop it."

She reluctantly agrees to have the AIDS awareness program included in the training.

The trainees are taught how to mix fabric paints to make colors; how to use leaves, twigs, and feathers to create patterns on fabric; and how to embroider. The final project is a painted and embroidered "story-square" in memory of a person from the crafter's family who died of AIDS. The nine-inch squares depict the deceased family member in a happy setting, doing something he or she enjoyed. In the safety of the workshop environment, each participant is able to admit that someone they know died of AIDS. The story-squares show boys playing soccer, singing, or hunting, some show women cooking or holding their children. EMBO Craft assembles the story-squares into quiltlike wall hangings that are taken to the International AIDS conference held in Durban in July 2000. The hangings are magnificent. The training is a great success. I am now sure there are sufficient skills and confidence to get a sewing club and micro-enterprise launched. Zulus must love to prove me wrong.

True to their hierarchical social order, Zulus gravitate together in formal groups and organizations. Post-apartheid, with the mandate of democratic self-governance, Zulu organizations are expected to write a constitution, elect leaders, and keep meeting minutes in addition to conducting the business at hand. iNkosi, anxious that his people progress, joins us at our first sewing club meeting, thus giving royal sanction to the process. Miss D is appointed acting chairperson for the day. The four-hour meeting begins with a great debate over how many people will be allowed in the club. About twenty people are present. The conversation focuses on analyzing the skill level and suitability of tribal members who might desire admittance. I suggest that anyone who wants to join should be allowed to join. They don't think that's a very good idea. They want to decide who can join. The who-and-how-many-can-join debate continues. I try to steer the conversation toward the issues at hand. What is the club going to produce? How will the items be priced? Who will buy the supplies? Each time after I speak the conversation returns to who and how many may join. Patience, I tell myself, let them move forward in their own way. I excuse myself from the meeting. I really do have other things I need to accomplish.

Later, Miss D reports that although the debate regarding membership continued, she was able to push the agenda forward to the selection of officers. Two people elected to club offices were not present at the meeting, so they will have to confirm their acceptance at the next meeting, scheduled for the following week. That meeting comes and goes—debate on membership continues. They decide on membership dues: ten rand ($1) per person. The treasurer asks me to hold the dues since no one else has a bank account. "What are the dues for?" I ask. "We haven't decided," she replies. No discussion on the more substantive issues occurs, but they select a club name.

I do not intervene. I want to see what they can do on their own.

Over the next two months, I attend two of their weekly meetings; Miss D attends all of them. The meetings are held in an old stone building on the grounds of St. Vincent's mission. Originally a horse stable, it has been converted into a meeting hall through a grant from WILD and work by Amafa. It's a ten-minute walk from my house, so I can come and go easily. Debate over the number of members allowed into the club fades along with the weekly attendance. The meeting size shrinks to ten people and they can't decide what to make. Some want to make pinafores, a cross between a housecoat and an apron. They are very popular with Zulu women. Some want to make school uniforms; some want to make personal items for their families. Squabbles break out among members, bickering over who should do what. Five people attend the ninth meeting. Nothing has been produced. Clearly, we don't have a success here. The Christmas and summer holidays approach. Everything stops in South Africa from early December until mid-January. I will consider what to do over the break and try again early in 2001.

Respecting their need for autonomy is one thing, but I'm not doing anyone a favor by letting the group flounder. I interview a few members privately. The group has deteriorated into an "us against them" feud—each side placing blame for why things can't get done. I had let months go by with no productive results. Miss D tells me that in most groups a few people do all the work, but when it's time to "cut the cake," everybody has her hand out. I ask advice from EMBO Craft's senior trainer; she has a lot of experience with rural craft initiatives. In her experience, groups larger than five or six rarely work. There is not enough individual accountability and there are too many issues with personalities. I don't need to be hit over the head. It is time to take charge.

I ask Miss D to organize a special meeting of all potential members of the sewing club. Maybe I expected too much too quickly. Maybe I am not evaluating the situation, seeing it from their perspective. I will ask them what they want for themselves, not force small business start-ups on them. I open the discussion.

Crafts, Crops, and Capitalism 139

"I am not here to tell you what to do with your lives. I am here for two years to help you reach the goals you want for yourselves. To help you have a better life. Tell me, please, what can I help you get in your life that you don't have?"

"I will like better clothes and clothes for my children."

"I will like electricity and a gas stove."

"I will like glass for my windows. The dust is terrible."

Not unreasonable requests.

"You know that the government will not give you these things and I cannot give you these things. But if you earn money, you can buy these things for yourself. Is there anything you can do to earn money?"

"Sew and make crafts for sale." They know how to give the answer I am looking for.

"You have been in club meetings for many months. Why did no one make anything for sale?"

"We do not have money to buy materials."

That problem never came up before. Thus, the beginning of WILD's microlending program.

Vance is due to arrive in a few days. A microlending program has been in his thoughts from the beginning. After some brainstorming, Vance designs a comprehensive self-help organization for all of our community participation projects. He wants name-brand identity to promote our initiatives and generate enthusiasm for our training. WILD will host a celebration to launch the organization before a communitywide assembly. We will distribute T-shirts printed with the organization's name to all members of the tribal council and pencils stamped with the name to all schoolchildren. Now all we have to do is to select the name, make the T-shirts, and order the pencils. Vance thinks we should be able to get it done in a week or two and launch the program shortly thereafter. Get a clue, Oh Great White Idea Generator.

"This is Zululand. Selecting the name will take weeks. You do not appreciate what we are dealing with."

"They can easily do it in a week. How difficult can it be to come up with a name?"

"You're going to find out."

We meet with Miss D and iNkosi and ask them for a name. They say the tribal council should select the name. iNkosi will bring it up at the next tribal council meeting a week from Wednesday.

"Great," says Vance. "Call me with the name on Wednesday and I'll order the pencils."

I'll bet a $1,000 that doesn't happen.

The tribal council meeting comes and goes—no name.

iNkosi reports, "The tribal council did not have time to discuss it."

"Why don't you and Miss D select a name? We need to get this going."

"No, it is better if the tribal council selects the name. I will put it on the agenda for the council meeting next week."

"Okay, we can wait."

The next tribal council meeting comes and goes. No word from iNkosi or Miss D. I ask for a meeting with them to discuss the progress of our projects. At that meeting, I ask about the name.

iNkosi says, "Perhaps at the next council meeting we will discuss it."

"It has been four weeks. We need the name so we can make the T-shirts and print pencils in time for Vance and Maggie's next visit. The three of us must decide on a name."

iNkosi doesn't want to do that. "It isn't my place. The name should be decided by the council."

"They have had four weeks to do it. You know I want to work with the tribal council, but they also have to work with me. You can blame me if they get upset. The name must be a word that non-Zulu speakers can pronounce. A word with a lot of click sounds won't do."

Miss D suggests Impumelelo. It means success.

"Great, Impumelelo it will be."

Miss D says, "The full name should be Impumelelo yeSandlwana, which means Success for the Community of Isandlwana."

"Done. I will give the name to Vance so he can order the pencils. Now we have to find a place to buy the T-shirts."

Miss D suggests that the women in the craft group create a design for the T-shirts and hand print them. Great. We will give a T-shirt to each member of the tribal council, members of the various projects, and the principals at each school, about 100 total. We need 3,000 pencils, one for each student. I locate a T-shirt wholesaler in Durban and persuade them to supply the T-shirts. Six women, with Miss D's supervision, make crude stencils and hand paint the T-shirts.

In a communitywide meeting, we present the T-shirts and announce our microlending program. We ask the community to join with us so that those who are willing to work can work for themselves. We are open for business. The hinges aren't pulled off my door by people charging in for loans. That's okay. Like the Marines, all we need are a few good women. Miss D explains that most Zulus don't like to work for themselves. They don't see themselves as entrepreneurs, and they like the comfort of having someone tell them what to do. Understandable. Under apartheid, blacks were excluded from positions of management or power. We'll start with what we have, the sewers and crafters.

WILD allocates 2,000 rand for the sewing-group lending fund. Miss D and I discuss a maximum amount for each loan. We don't want to make the loans too large or they will be difficult to repay. A 500-rand limit is prudent and still sufficient to allow for a reasonable profit potential. We can provide four loans, maybe more. I design a loan application form that, when filled out, becomes a mini–business plan. It has questions such as What do you want to make? What do you need to make it? How many items do you want to make? How much material or supplies do you need to make that many? As part of EMBO Craft's workshop, forty-two women and two men rotated through a How to Start Your Own Small Business working session. Each participant received a solar-powered calculator and simple instructions, written in Zulu, on how to calculate costs and profit.

I announce that loans are available for small groups only, no more than five to six people per group. Each member of the group must sign the loan document, thereby accepting responsibility for the loan. The loans are interest free. The groups will have ample time for repayment.

"What happens if we do not repay the loans?" they ask.

"We will announce at a tribal council meeting which groups repaid the loans and which didn't. WILD can reloan money to other groups only if the money is paid back. If a group doesn't repay the loan, the community suffers," I tell them.

The women don't like that idea at all. They try to convince me that larger groups are better. Avoiding accountability is easier in larger groups. I hold my ground.

"In four months, no one has produced anything for sale— not even a plan to make anything. It is easier for you to schedule meetings and agree on a plan in smaller groups with no more than five or six per group. Miss D will assist those who want to apply for loans. Please organize your groups and come here Friday." Clear and concise. I leave believing I have the situation under control.

Life in Zululand gives me a graduate degree in patience. Working with the sewing group adds another dimension: it elevates my practice of tolerance to a spiritual experience. Three groups arrive to apply for the loans. One group wants to make school uniforms to sell. Trying to get information from them for filling out the loan application form reminds me of the old Laurel and Hardy joke about the baseball player named Hoose. You probably know the joke. The conversation goes thusly:

"How many uniforms do you want to make?"

"As many as we can sell."

"How many people do you think will buy the uniforms?"

"Depends on how many people have money to buy."

"How much will each school uniform cost to make?"

"I do not know."

"How much material will it take to make a blouse?"

"About this much," pulling at her blouse.

"How much is that?"

Looking at me like I am dull-witted, she repeats, "*This much,*" pulling at her blouse more vigorously.

I need a new approach.

"How many meters of fabric does it take to make a blouse?"

A blank stare.

I turn to Miss D. "I think the groups need help with the forms. I will leave it in your capable hands." I leave the group to cope with the challenges of capitalism.

Miss D and I agree that the group members should gather the information to fill out the forms rather than us doing it for them. That process takes three weeks. With three applications completed, we are ready to present the money. No group needs more than 500 rand. At the next sewing club meeting, we distribute the loan money.

"Why only 500 rand?"

Miss D and I explain that no group needs more than 500 rand and a larger loan will be difficult to repay. We show them the calculations on their application forms.

"But you said 2,000 rand."

"We have 2,000 rand for the all the loans but only 500 for each loan, so we can give out four loans."

"Why did you say 2,000 rand?"

"I said we had a total of 2,000 rand. That is four 500-rand loans."

"Why won't you give us the 2,000 rand?"

No amount of rational explanation can dissuade one participant from insisting that the loan should be 2,000 rand.

A few months later, a psychologist who has studied the thought and communication styles of people raised in oral- rather than written-tradition cultures informs me that in oral-tradition cultures the right side of the brain, the intuitive side, is more developed. In written-tradition cultures the left side of the brain, the more linear and analytical side, is better developed. The two types of cultures receive and process information differently. She tells me about people who cannot count and do not understand the concept of numbers but can inspect a herd of cows and know if they all are present. That's my problem. I need to think with my right brain. I am thinking like a left-brained Westerner.

Each group wants to make items familiar to them: pinafores, school uniforms, and beaded collars, rather than the startlingly attractive story-square quilts or patchwork items. I think story quilts will appeal to tourists and be a great success. They are different, lightweight, easy to pack, and very African. I explain that the items they are trained to make are perfect to sell at the lodge and the visitors center. They don't want to make them. Okay, I let them choose.

The pinafore group likes the pinafores they make so much that they refuse to sell them.

I explain, "The reason you start a business is to make money so you can afford the things you said you wanted."

"Yes, but we like the pinafores. We should not have to sell them."

"How are you going to pay back the loan?" Silence. "If you sell the pinafores you can pay back the loan and have enough leftover to buy more material to make pinafores for yourselves."

"We want to keep these. Perhaps," one group member suggests, "we buy the pinafores from ourselves and use that money to repay the loans."

Try explaining the math on that transaction and why it won't work to their advantage. With patience and perseverance, Miss D is able explain the intricacies of cash flow. They eventually sell the pinafores, make others, and repay the loan in full.

The women who applied for a loan to make school uniforms change their minds and makes pinafores instead. They have difficulty selling the pinafores. It's basic supply and demand; there are too many available for sale.

"Why didn't you make the school uniforms as you said?"

"We tried to get the school uniform material but it wasn't the right color. Pinafores were easier."

"Applying for a loan to make one thing and then, without consultation, making another is not right. The loan application is a formal document. You can't accept money to make one thing and then make another." That idea does not compute.

"Why is it wrong to make pinafores? You said we could make what we want—the other group made pinafores."

Accept what is, Carol, and try again next time. For now there are pinafores to sell.

Miss D and I offer suggestions on how they can get the pinafores to another market. They aren't really interested. What they want is another loan so they can make more pinafores because they don't have anything to do. They have spent all of their money on fabric for the first batch of pinafores.

"You haven't been able to sell the pinafores you already have. Why do you think it would be a good idea to make more?"

"The pinafores will sell. We need something to do now."

"How about making patchwork or story-squares? I know you could sell those." Silence.

The pinafores do eventually sell, or they sell other things, because they repay the loan. Their financial records are so poor that it is difficult to know what happened, and they are less than forthcoming with an explanation. I comfort myself that we are at least making progress.

Twice each year the local municipal government sponsors an agricultural fair. There are contests for the best animals, produce, and crafts. Three sewers submit patchwork vests, pillow covers, and story-squares for the contests and win first prize. They are bursting with pride when they show me their certificates. I am convinced that this will give them the confidence to make the items for sale. I am wrong. Still, I make suggestions for story-squares. The Zulu names for each month of the year are based on activities that occur during that month. Making a Zulu calendar wall hanging out of the story-squares will be fabulous. No takers. Miss D makes a story quilt and sells it for 500 rand. At a crafters' meeting, she shows them the money, more than most have ever had at one time, to prove she sold it and that we are telling the truth. I have an order from an American for several story quilts. The women will not make them and will not give reasons why. I ask Miss D what the problem is—"Lazy," she says. That doesn't make sense. They will produce familiar items for local consumption, but they won't expose themselves to the outside world of commerce and tourism.

Similar to Native American communities in the United States, Zulu communities are disconnecting from their heritage, from their old stories and traditions. Rural Zulus are ridiculed by their urban brothers for holding on to traditional culture. Society demands modernization, but with few resources or skills to make it happen, rural Zulus become disenfranchised. Perhaps cultivating a positive identity with their culture and pride in their traditional crafts will encourage the women to reach beyond their safe enclosure.

EMBO Craft, like many community-centered programs, is justifiably concerned that if the Zulus abandon their roots and heritage, there will not only be an irreplaceable cultural loss for South Africa, but the loss will also lead to further breakdown in the social order, generating despair and more violence. EMBO Craft's focus, with WILD's involvement, builds on the assumption that indigenous culture must play an active role in linking people to their environment. EMBO Craft develops a workshop, in part funded by WILD, which combines traditional storytelling with nature conservation awareness and craft skills training. It is a brilliant concept.

Most of the stories in traditional Zulu culture are linked to the environment. There are stories of floods, famine, drought, and disease. Each story can be used as a springboard to discuss environmental issues. We will gather the crafters; the old grannies, called *gogos*; and the young people of the community for a storytelling workshop. We serve lunch and make it a party.

A crafter is assigned to each *gogo*. The crafters are asked to draw a story-square depicting the *gogo's* story while a scribe writes it down. The EMBO Craft leader tries to guide the *gogos* toward stories with environmental implications, but her approach is a little too subtle. Either that or the *gogos* have ideas of their own. For the first hour, each story we hear is about wars, killing, and girls maintaining their virginity. Not exactly what we are looking for, but an interesting insight into Zulu culture.

The *gogos'* stories are wonderful. Their recall is amazing. Each remembers the king and iNkosi who ruled when different clans feuded, and each describes in detail all of the bloody consequences. One *gogo* tells the story of why she hasn't eaten chicken in seventy-five years. When she was a little girl, a family from another part of the tribal area came onto her family's land to shoot birds. Her family resented the territorial encroachment and retaliated by killing game on the offending family's turf. The feud escalated until family members were killing each other. It lasted until there were no men left to kill or be killed.

In an effort to shift to stories with obvious environmental themes, Miss D volunteers a tale about illness from polluted water. iNkosi tells a story he remembers from his grandmother about drought and famine. Soon the rest of the *gogos* remember stories that relate to the need to protect water, pastureland, and trees. We talk about how overgrazing and tree removal causes erosion, water loss, and poor crops, and how disease is caused by contaminated water. We explain that if they care for the environment, they care for themselves.

We talk with the young people who came to hear the stories. We talk about how cans, bottles, paper, and the official "flower of

Africa"—plastic shopping bags—strewn about the countryside send a message to tourists that South Africans have no pride in their home and therefore in themselves. Although there is no garbage collection in the area, the community has informal land-fills and most families burn what little refuse they have. We organize a community pride day. School teams, carrying large trash bags, clean up around the schools and the "downtown" area. Students organize cleanups in their local neighborhoods. Shortly after cleanup day, Miss D and I watch as a child throws a piece of paper on the ground. Another girl bends down to retrieve the paper. She carries it to a rubbish bin near the visitors center. We both thank the girl. As Zulu villages go, this one remains remarkably clean.

The story-squares made by the crafters from the *gogos* stories are colorful, fun, and engaging. EMBO Craft mounts the story-squares onto fabric, creating small wall hangings to sell in their shop near Durban. The proceeds help fund the training and sub-sidize the cost of craft supplies used by the women. We tell the crafters that if they make additional squares on the subject of their choice, EMBO Craft will purchase them. We hope that this will provide the necessary encouragement for the women to pro-duce story-squares for sale. It doesn't.

The only explanation I have for their extreme reluctance to produce these items for sale is an entrenched societal fear of change. Don't be different, it causes trouble; don't reach outside the boundaries of the tribe, it's unknown and that makes it unsafe. Change doesn't come easily to people excluded from the social and political change process. Willingness to change emerges most readily from a foundation of confidence and trust in one's abilities and environment. Perhaps through encourage-ment, example, small steps, and small successes, the women will develop the confidence to choose change, because without change their lives cannot get better.

After we start the microlending program for the sewers, a group of poultry producers approaches Miss D to ask for a loan to expand their business. Broiler chickens grow from egg to ready-to-eat bird in six weeks. These chickens are increasingly offered for sale in the area since fewer households raise their own chickens. We interview the poultry growers. As they answer our questions, it becomes clear that the growers are losing money on every chicken they raise. They spend twenty-seven rand buying the chicks and feeding them to adulthood, but they sell the chickens for twenty-two rand. No wonder they need a loan. Miss D and I agree that she should teach a class to the poultry growers on business basics: calculating costs and managing profit. The problem for WILD is that the chickens are raised in an over-crowded shed without light or air. WILD, in good conscious, cannot fund the project until the poultry producers locate a better living environment for the chicks. I turn the situation over to Miss D and await further developments.

Two months later Miss D completes a training course with three groups that want loans to raise broiler chickens. The groups learn how to raise the chicks profitably, understand the financial requirements, and have suitable facilities for the chicks. It is time for me to inspect the sites and approve the loans. Two groups built acceptable chicken coops. Miss D and I drive to the *muzi* of the third poultry grower. We are greeted by the group's members and escorted to one of the *rondavals*. The people who lived in the *rondaval* have squeezed in with other family members, vacating their home. Voila! Instant chicken lodging. It isn't much bigger than the shed, with one tiny window for air and light. Can I tell the people who lived in it that it isn't good enough for chickens?

Not likely! All three groups receive loans.

Building on our successes, we expand the microlending program to include the lending of garden tools. Community gardens are vital in this area to provide a nutritious, affordable food supply. Sustainable cultures are rarely built on white bread and Kool-Aid, favorites of the Zulus. Each garden must be fenced to keep out the free-ranging goats and cattle. The South African Department of Agriculture supplies fencing for a limited number of community gardens. WILD buys spades, hoes, pitchforks and watering cans for four community gardens, one in each ward. We present the tools at a communitywide tribal meeting. We also supply each garden group with a logbook to record lending of the tools. Knowing it's easy to misuse things that are free, we emphasize the importance of caring for the tools. We tell each garden group in front of the assembled community that the tools are on loan provided 1.) All tools are kept available, i.e. aren't stolen; 2.) They are kept clean and in good repair; 3.) They are used in the gardens. If those terms are not met, we will award the tools to another garden.

Three weeks later Miss D and I visit the gardens for an inspection. At our first stop, the chairperson of the garden, beaming with pride, brings us the tools still covered in their original protective wrappers.

"You see, the tools are in excellent condition."

"I am very pleased that the tools are clean, but the tools must be used."

"Yes, Missus. The garden is not fenced so we cannot plant."

"I thought you had a fence from the Department of Agriculture."

"Yes, but we do not have permission from the Department of Agriculture extension agent to put it up."

"Why do you need permission to put up the fence?"

"The agent must approve."

A downside of hierarchical societies. Make a note: get permission. The second garden is good to go. People are in the fields breaking up the ground. The third garden has a small problem. They installed a Department of Agriculture fence, but a large part of it was stolen and resurrected at a nearby *muzi*. The chairperson of the garden complained to the local *induna*, but the purloined fence protected a *muzi* of the *induna*'s family. The gardeners are awaiting action.

The fourth garden has a very ambitious chairperson. The gardeners dug a water collection pond, lined it with rocks, and dug reticulation trenches from the pond to the garden. It is a masterpiece. This garden has not received one of the Department of Agriculture's fences. Their fence posts and crossbars are made from shrubs, weeds, branches, and bits of tin and other discarded items bound together with twine made from braided grass. Fences have been made like this for millennia. What a wonderful site. A few months later I am brokenhearted to hear that kids stole part of the fence to burn as fuel. Miss D organizes a community meeting to ask that the fence be respected. The gardeners and their families depend on the gardens for food. The repaired fence remains intact.

The Department of Agriculture sponsors "Farmers Day" in the tribal area. The agriculture extension worker and her associates ask the 150 attendees to gather around two demonstration plots to view the glories of modern agriculture. The department planted a plot of corn the "modern" way next to a plot of corn planted the old-fashioned way. Indeed, the plot planted the modern way is more abundant. She explains that to achieve these amazing results one must:

1.) Put an all-purpose herbicide across the field to kill everything growing.
2.) Take a stick, poke a hole in the ground, put in the corn seed, add fertilizer and growth hormone, then cover it up. Water and wait for it to sprout.
3.) Once sprouted, dust the seedling with pesticide and more fertilizer and let it grow.

Voila, a generous crop. What they don't mention is the cost of the chemicals—far more than the people can afford and more than the value of the crop, not to mention that the pesticides and herbicides pollute the surface water and eventually decrease the viability of the land.

It appears that the Department of Agriculture or the extension worker is pimping for the chemical companies without considering, or perhaps even understanding, the consequences. I am furious. Vance suggests that I hire permaculture trainers to conduct a workshop on natural gardening methods. A nonprofit called Gardens for Africa specializes in training rural and periurban people in environmentally sound, inexpensive gardening techniques. I arrange a four-day workshop for representatives from seven community gardens. Dom, the trainer, teaches composting, water capture and control techniques, wind protection, intercropping to limit pest damage, and the planting of "sacrifice" plants to attract pests away from the produce. The gardeners take to permaculture training like ducks to water.

I've never seen anybody pick up on training so quickly. The older gardeners say it reminds them of how their parents and grandparents gardened. Within days, the gardens have changed. The gardeners collect plastic bottles, poke tiny holes in the bottoms, and arrange them along the crop rows. The tiny holes allow the water to leak slowly into the ground. I laugh out loud when I drive up to a garden and see a bumper crop of soda bottles growing in neatly planted rows. Finally, an easy success. But hold on, Tonto! It's too early for a self-congratulatory happy hour. The Department of Agriculture is not going to take this lying down.

The agriculture extension worker hears about the training and is quite annoyed that we did not ask her permission. Intercropping is planting alternating rows of vegetables rather than rows of all of one vegetable. Varying the rows helps prevent the spread of plant diseases and pests. When she sees the intercropping, she tells the gardeners to pull it out and replant one kind of vegetable in neat little rows. She threatens one gardener, telling her to remove the compost pile or lose her support of the garden. She tells another gardener that he has to buy fertilizer from her. Using manure isn't acceptable. Petty little bureaucratic tyrant. I bet she gets a kickback on the fertilizer sales.

I ask Miss D what we can do to stop her. She says iNkosi should have a meeting with the extension worker's boss. iNkosi says he will set up a meeting, but he does not. I ask again. Once again he says he will but doesn't. I ask Miss D if she will set up the meeting. She says no, that would not be right. Finally, Miss D suggests that she and iNkosi should meet with the extension worker before going to her boss. Miss D sets up that meeting. In classic Zulu style, the extension worker cancels at the last minute. Agree to anything, then give last minute excuses why you can't attend. If the meeting never occurs, the process can't move forward. Again, Miss D sets up a meeting and again the extension worker cancels. All the while, her threats to the gardeners continue.

Through their extension workers, the Department of Agriculture supplies the gardens with seeds, plants, and fencing, so the extension worker wields a lot of "threatening power." One gardener suggests that they grow half the garden the way Dom taught and the other half the way the Department of Agriculture said to do it. Peace at any price.

I reply, "You should be able to choose how you want to grow your garden—any way that you think is the best for you."

The gardener demurs, "Yes, we like what Dom taught us, but that is the way with government."

One old granny fights back with classic passive avoidance. The *gogo* agrees to do exactly what the extension worker asks and walks away smiling. Nothing gets changed. On the worker's next visit, when the *gogo* is asked why she hasn't ripped out the inter-cropping, the *gogo* tells her the gardeners have been sick and "Next time we will do it." On the extension worker's next visit, when the intercropping and compost remain, the *gogo* says the gardeners have been too busy gathering dried aloe for fuel. On her next visit, when they haven't purchased the recommended fertilizer and pesticides, the *gogo* says it is because they don't have enough money. "Would the extension worker help out the old people and supply the garden with fertilizer at no charge? We are very poor." The *gogo* radiates a triumphant smile; all the while, the permaculture garden is growing nicely.

I am surprised by the lack of movement on iNkosi's part. I continue to press our case, asking iNkosi and Miss D to take the problem to the Department of Agriculture's regional managers, but no dice. No meetings occur, or none that they tell me about. I'll only push so far. If they don't have the will or the inclination to deal with the issue directly rather than simply agree how wrong the extension worker's behavior is, then they will have to live with the consequences. I suspect the extension worker has ties to influential people and wields power behind the scenes, but

I will never find out by asking. Clan and family ties in rural Zululand hold heavy sway over who does what for whom.

The Department of Health unwittingly joins in our cause. Outbreaks of illness from water contaminated with fertilizer and pesticide runoff has the Department of Health issuing warnings not to use chemicals. Miss D is working on a plan to get the local Department of Health to talk to the Department of Agriculture. Patience, Carol, it will happen.

Chapter 15: Houses as Gifts

I KNEW LIVING IN A CULTURE SO DRAMATICALLY DIFFERENT from my own would have its challenges, but I underestimated their magnitude. I remember how my early weeks in the village were filled with delays and disappointments as I struggled to repair equipment and obtain services. Still, a year into my stay, each day continues to include some event that obstructs progress. But these frustrations pale in comparison to the soap opera of cross-cultural interactions that play out over the course of building two houses, one for iNkosi and one for WILD. First, iNkosi must select a building site and have the site location approved by the tribal council. For logistical and financial reasons, it is better to build the houses next to each other, and for safety reasons I want to be near the eyes and ears of attentive neighbors, not stranded in a remote part of the tribal area. The process of selecting the homesites unearths old power struggles between family factions. One side of the royal family wants iNkosi's house (and by default WILD's) built on an isolated hill away from the main flow of activity but near their *muzi* and thus, by association, under their influence. iNkosi selects other sites but cannot gain tribal council approval, so he does what he does best: outlasts their opposition. After inconvenient absences from tribal meetings and delayed responses to tribal council requests, in late May 2000 the royal family and tribal council agree to site the houses next to each other on abandoned cornfields near the lodge.

Next order of business: hire a builder. Everyone I speak to who has used a local contractor has nothing good to say about them. They took much too long, forgot to hook up the sewer so the plumbing backed up, the roof blew off, and on and on. It is not encouraging. Many of the builders I interview jack up the price threefold when they discover Americans are building the houses—after all, aren't all Americans rich?

I locate a builder who lives two hours away. Luke, an Afrikaner, comes with good references and reasonable prices. The house site, an elevated field near the lodge visible from the battle-field, is a conspicuous part of the landscape. To preserve the visual identity of the area, we design a house for WILD that will be built from cinder block, plastered over with cement, and painted to look like mud brick with a thatch roof. To be polite and include iNkosi in the decision-making process, I ask for his design preferences.

Hindsight is a beautiful thing. Rather than placing the burden of decision on iNkosi's shoulders, I should have presented it as a gift: "We are building this luxurious home for you. I know you will enjoy it." I would have avoided asking for input he was ill prepared to provide or forcing him to seek council from people even less qualified to offer appropriate guidance. Instead, I open Pandora's box with "What kind of house would you like, iNkosi?" That question initiates my diplomatic training course, emersion style.

I assume that if someone offered to build a house for me, especially one that is much nicer than anything I've ever lived in, I would just shut up and say thank you. That reasoning fails to recognize the powerful symbolic and emotional implications of building a house for a newly appointed tribal chief. The kind of house we build for him defines his stature in the community and the value we place on him. The flashier, the more Western the house, the more we respect him and the more respect he deserves—a concept not foreign to the developed world. I am what I own, Zulu style. Wall Street values, misplaced human values, are haunting me even here.

iNkosi wants a Western-style house rather than a more traditional *muzi* configuration. Luke says that building one house rather than several *rondaval*-like structures is significantly less expensive. I look through design books and select three floor plans that suit iNkosi's needs and stay within a reasonable budget. I give the designs to iNkosi. He cannot visualize how the houses will look and will not approve any of them. I ask if he knows of a house that is similar to what he wants. I am burying myself by the minute. iNkosi drives me to the house of a Zulu politician and businessman. It is a faux-Mediterranean monstrosity made of brick with a tile roof that would be an expensive, hideous eyesore in the tribal area. I'm in a real jam. iNkosi's preferences should be included in selecting the house design, but with each bit of input, the house plans become more inappropriate, time consuming, and expensive.

I am managing the process badly; but like a boulder rolling downhill, once moving, it's difficult to stop. I ask iNkosi what he wants and then tell him why he can't have it. The process is exhausting me and frustrating the builder. Goodness knows what kind of pressure iNkosi feels. I have to become more proactive.

Luke and I select a plan that approximates the inside design of the house iNkosi showed us, a small four-bedroom, two-bath with attached garage. Like the WILD house, his will be constructed with blocks, plastered with cement, and painted to look like mud with a thatch roof. iNkosi's house is larger and more expensive than the house WILD is building for itself. I hope this will appease him and he will let us get on with the task of building the houses. Wrong again.

He insists that he does not want a thatch roof. He wants a modern roof, it is better. For those not familiar with thatch, it is fabulous. Thatched homes are open and spacious with a wonderful scent of sweetgrass. They are cool in the summer and well insulated in the winter. I ask Miss D why iNkosi is so resistant to thatch. She implies that poor black people use thatch—if it is so wonderful why don't white people have it? Sweet Mother of God, is a thatch roof a racial issue? Despite my frustrations I do understand why iNkosi thinks thatch is inferior. For a thatch roof to properly drain it must have a forty-five-degree pitch. In a house that is twenty-five feet by fifty feet, the peak of the ceiling is about eighteen feet high with open beams. If the pitch is not steep enough to allow the thatch to drain, the roofs leak and rot. Most poor homes don't pitch the roofs adequately, so after a year or two the roofs collapse. White people don't use thatch because properly installed, it is more expensive than traditional roofing.

The WILD Foundation wants thatch on its house and the upscale lodge has a thatch roof. His roof needs to be thatch to blend with the surroundings. This is ridiculous, but I don't need an international crisis, so I call in a consultant who is well versed in the Zulu culture.

After a lot of talk, patience, and persuading, iNkosi agrees to a thatch roof, but he wants The WILD Foundation house built first so he can see what it will look like before his house is built. Will this ever end? Both houses have to be built simultaneously to coordinate materials delivery, construction workers on-site, equipment rental, and so forth. He asks, "How will I know if I approve of the house until I see it?" I assure him we will build a very nice house for him. He reluctantly agrees.

I struggle to recognize iNkosi's subtle cultural signals. I strain to understand when his seemingly consenting words really mean "no way, thank you" or when he agrees in order to avoid conflict even though he never intends to follow through. Persistence works in his favor when dealing with the royal family and tribal council, but it drives me up a wall. People tell me that I am tenacious, but iNkosi retires the shirt. He just never gives in. Since direct confrontation can get a person killed in Zululand, one of the ways Zulus succeed is by politely outlasting their opponent. In addition, iNkosi's image among his people is still being formed. His effectiveness as a leader is on the line. If he fails to get his way on something so obvious as the design of his house, especially when dealing with a woman, he will be labeled weak, and weak *amakosi* don't live long.

Intellectually I understand his issues, but emotionally they push all my buttons. Working in this very rural area with incompetent systems and unprofessional business practices is difficult, and he is making it more so. Can't he just be grateful and get out of the way? I think I am building two houses. I am actually building a relationship across cultures that can influence the lives of thousands of people.

Luke sets up a work camp on the construction site and will stay until the project is complete, estimated to be six months. He brings a few trusted employees, but will hire locals for most of the labor. I have to introduce Luke to the tribal council before construction can begin. Nothing happens here without informing the tribal council. We coordinate a date for his introduction and ask the tribal council to start the selection process for his local labor.

My problems are just beginning. Luke is a very nice man but a lousy manager, and he comes with some deeply entrenched attitudes and practices leftover from apartheid. Most of the construction is done by hand: digging trenches and fence postholes, mixing cement, and laying blocks. Luke lends out tools to the crew and then pitches a fit when half the tools are missing the next morning. I suggest a logbook. "Stealing is expected," he says, "That's what they do."

The block and cement vendors deliver nothing on time. The work inches along. Eventually the foundations are poured. When the interior walls are about five feet high, iNkosi tells Luke that he doesn't like the layout and will Luke please move the walls. Luke comes to me, furious. The concrete foundation is thicker under the internal walls to support their weight. He will have to redo the entire foundation. Confronting iNkosi directly isn't working, it isn't the Zulu way. In Zulu style everything is done indirectly through others by innuendo. I much prefer clear direct interchange, but if the situation warrants, I can adapt.

I speak to Miss D about the expenses incurred by changing house plans. I say we hope iNkosi will like his new home, but with changes and delays we may not get the job done before we run out of money. Wouldn't that be a pity, we do so want iNkosi to have a home in the tribal area. I ask if she thinks he would prefer to remain near his family in Ladysmith. There are no more comments about the walls.

I don't blame iNkosi or his copious advisors for the difficulties. iNkosi is a pawn of the tribe's expectations. They are testing his skill at getting as much as he can. Still, I take his objections and requests personally. In comparison to iNkosi and the tribal members, I have abundant comfort and security. Every time I deny a request, I feel cheap or selfish. I need to find my own balance in this process and to put what WILD is doing and what I have to offer in context. One of the greatest mistakes anyone can make in relationships that span unequal financial ground is for one to give too much, or give it in a way that makes the receiver feel disempowered. I also understand the Zulu mind-set that whites, foreigners, and Americans in particular have an endless supply of money, so why not ask—they have it to give.

To be honest, part of my frustration comes from a monster lurking in the dark of my psyche: fear for my safety. I am a white woman alone in a Zulu village. I am afraid to annoy iNkosi and lose his protection. He sets the tone in the village. The Mangwe-Buthanani tribe must keep me safe. Every time I go to town white businesspeople—the bank teller, the telephone service representative, the grocery store clerk—comment on how surprised they are that I am alive and still living "out there." They won't even drive out to visit, it is too dangerous. Many years of violence and conflict have taken their toll on the collective mind-set of South Africans, both black and white. I do not believe iNkosi would turn his back on me or not make every effort to keep me safe, but I don't want to even think it is a possibility. My fear traps me, and my reluctance to confront the situation allows it to escalate. Where is the faith and courage that got me here? Missing in action, at least for the moment.

Theft at the work site increases. I make a few suggestions for curbing the theft, but Afrikaner men aren't any more willing to listen to women than are Zulu males. Luke grumbles about losing materials but is ineffective at stopping it. One day Luke's assistant, Steve, noticeably agitated, knocks on my door asking to use the phone. One of the workers Steve brought with him was accosted at gunpoint by a tribal member. The worker was told that he had until sunset to get out of town or he would be shot. I am speechless. Get out of town by sunset?! How did John Wayne end up here? The severity of the situation breaks through its absurdity. Steve tells me that the local man threatened the out-sider because the local wants his job. Outsiders aren't welcome in this area. How can these people be so petty and violent? I leave to find iNkosi and Miss D; Steve calls the police. The stage is set for a lesson on jumping to conclusions.

I inform Miss D of the death threat. She contacts iNkosi and follows up with the police. With diligent investigations by iNkosi, Miss D, and her band of boys, the truth is told. Luke's laborer used the accusation of resentment of outsiders as a cover-up. A generator and an air compressor, two very expensive items, were stolen. Luke believes it is an inside job and blames the locals. He tells the Mangwe-Buthanani tribal members that they will not be paid until the generator and compressor are returned. The local people know Luke's "trusted" imported employees are the ringleaders responsible for the theft. Rather than turn the crooks in to their white boss, the locals take matters into their own hands. The situation is exposed, the generator and compres-sor are returned, and Luke fires his longtime employees. But trouble at the work site continues.

Early in the construction process, Luke tolerates some theft. We watch kids haul water jugs in our newly missing wheelbar-rows. At least we are saving their neck vertebrae, but it establishes a bad precedent. As the houses approach completion, the theft rate rises dramatically. The site becomes sort of a last-chance supply depot: get it now while materials last. Gone missing are large amounts of bricks, thatch polls, cement, tools, paint, and more.

In April 2001, when I return to Isandlwana after a few days absence, the cross-cultural saga gains another player. Luke informs me of a crippling level of theft at the construction site. I ask if he has any idea who is involved. He points across the way to the *sangoma's muzi*. A *sangoma* is a medicine man/woman/witch doctor/diviner. A few months ago Luke hired the *sangoma* to work as a laborer. A new *rondaval* is being erected with high-quality red bricks and pressure-treated thatch polls. Two of the *sangoma's* mud brick *rondavals* are covered with a fresh coating of cement. The scene is the visual equivalent of a Frank Lloyd Wright home in the middle of a shantytown. Luke wants to take a posse and retrieve the stolen goods. I strongly discourage him, afraid it will start real trouble, à la the Hatfields versus the McCoys, Zulu style. I don't need my neighbor the *sangoma* cursing me or playing dirty tricks. It is best to work through appropriate tribal channels.

Luke, his foreman, and I drive to Miss D's *muzi* to ask her advice. She says we should get the tribal policing forum representative who has legal authority in these matters. He can confront the alleged thief. We load my *bakkie* with Miss D, Luke, and his foreman to find Mr. Khomolo, the law in these parts. After a brief tour of the village, we locate Mr. K. He walks toward my truck carrying a cattle whip tied to a long stick. Men carry sticks as a symbol of authority and as a weapon. Eyeing the whip I envision some rather draconian behavior, but dismiss it as my imagination getting the best of me. Even so, I wish there were some way I could be left out of this tribunal. No such luck. We explain the situation to Mr. Khomolo. Everyone piles in to the *bakkie* once more (it's getting a little crowded in the back) to return to my neighbor the *sangoma's muzi*. When we arrive, the *sangoma's* wife tells us that he is conducting a ceremony at a distant *muzi*. The posse reloads in search of the perpetrator.

After some inquiry, we find the *muzi* where the *sangoma* officiates. I park my *bakkie* a respectful distance from the ceremony and wait for Mr. Khomolo, armed with his whip, to retrieve the *sangoma*. Mr. K returns with the *sangoma*, who carries a large kitchen knife. The *sangoma* was conducting a ritual of protection that required sacrificing a chicken.

I am not liking this one bit. My imagination takes over. I have fallen though a tear in the space-time continuum, transporting me back to a time when conflicts were settled man to man. Can I please go home now? I look around. No one else seems the slightest bit disturbed. A group of men join our little gathering, taking positions on either side of the *sangoma*. The group is decidedly split into two camps. At Mr. K's urging, the recently arrived men disperse and the rest of us stuff ourselves into the vehicle to return to the *sangoma's* homesite. Blessedly, someone relieves the *sangoma* of his knife before he climbs into the truck. On the way back to his *muzi*, Miss D suggests that we pick up the councilman for my area. It takes another half hour to get that accomplished, and the investigating party is finally assembled. We arrive at the *sangoma's muzi* and gather in front of the new brick and mortar *rondaval*. To an outsider it must look like a party is about to begin.

The *sangoma's* wife, a baby tied around her hips in traditional Zulu fashion, and his grandmother move sufficiently close to hear the conversation but not close enough to be considered part of the group. Everyone is very polite and courteous. Mr. K begins by asking about the *sangoma's* family and his health. He then explains why we are here. Will the *sangoma* please tell us where he got the new bricks? Luke thinks they might be his.

To put this in perspective, red bricks are extremely expensive by South African standards, costing three rand each in an area where a day's wage is twenty rand. We are the only construction site for many miles and probably the only site that has bricks for fifty miles. All of the buildings in the area are made of mud or cinder block. The *rondaval* in question began as a mud brick structure, changed to cinder block (most likely ours), then to red bricks. A pile of unused bricks near the *rondaval* is covered with heavy black construction plastic that costs twelve rand per meter, much more than a local could afford.

The conversation is in Zulu. Miss D periodically whispers a translation. No, the *sangoma* didn't steal these things. Steve told him he could have them. Conveniently for the *sangoma*, Steve is not here. There is much debate about whether or not Steve would have let the *sangoma* have the bricks. Luke weighs in that this scenario is impossible; the rest, being a little less absolute, agree it is highly unlikely. The conversation pauses occasionally to allow everyone to collect his or her thoughts. During these pauses, the assembled gaze up at the contested bricks enclosing the almost completed *rondaval*. Perhaps we await divine revelation? Luke's foreman leaves the group to look around the *muzi*. He returns reporting that thatch polls, tools, and wheelbarrows are hidden in a collapsing *rondaval* on the far side of the *muzi*. Will the *sangoma* please explain where those came from?

The wheelbarrows are indeed Luke's, but the *sangoma* thought that a man such as Luke would not need them anymore and since they are old, he decided to clean and repair them. The thatch polls are leftovers given to him by the thatch contractor. Why, then, Luke asks, did the thatch contractor run out of poles and have to go buy more, costing him time and money? The *sangoma* doesn't know why the contractor would do that. Maybe the contractor didn't like the poles and wanted new ones. As for the tools, he borrowed them so that he would be sure to have them when he worked for Luke at the site.

We stand in the *rondaval* for almost an hour. I am on an introspective Ferris wheel: at the top I think, "Isn't it wonderful how polite, courteous, and patient everyone is to amicably resolve this situation? How very civilized." At the bottom I despair, "We are totally wasting time. I'm bored and losing patience. I have things to do. Just tell the stupid thief that he has to return the stuff he stole and work off payment for at least part of the material he used. It's no wonder nothing gets done here!"

The dialogue continues in Zulu, but I sense a mood shift. Everyone seems to understand that the conversation is getting nowhere. We leave the *rondaval* and move to the plastic-covered stash of unused bricks. Mr. K seems impatient. I might argue that it is impossible for Zulus to be impatient. Impatience requires placing value on time, and that is missing here. Nevertheless, he tells the *sangoma* that we will stay until he admits that the bricks were not his to take. Mr. K's approach is to gently wear the *sangoma* down. The problem is that I am the one getting worn down. Just as Mr. K delivers his declaration, the *sangoma's* stooped-over, wrinkled-up *gogo*, who has disappeared into one of the *rondavals*, runs out, strafes the group with Zulu words, and ducks back into the *rondaval*. No one acknowledges her, but there is a slight smile on Miss D's downturned face. The conversation continues … and continues … and continues … The *gogo* darts out and again shouts the same phrase three times. More-obvious smiles break out on the faces of the assembled; the *sangoma* is noticeably disturbed. Mr. K pushes the *sangoma* to admit he took the bricks.

Finally, the *sangoma* admits the bricks are Luke's and that

Steve did not give him permission to take them, but the *sangoma* did not take them. Luke's workers stole the bricks and gave them to the *sangoma*. Luke asks, "Which workers?" The *sangoma* won't tell. Mr. K says if he doesn't tell, he will take the rap. The *sangoma*, for reasons unknown to me, also admits that Luke's workers stole paint and cement, leaving the loot with him until a pickup could be arranged. Can we enter his *rondaval* to get the paint? No, we can't. The *sangoma* says he could get into trouble if we went in. I try to figure out the logic. He admits he received stolen goods, admits, at least in part, what goods they are, but won't let us get them because he could get into trouble. Perhaps there is more stolen loot in the *rondaval*. Okay, will he get the paint? No, it is all gone. No one demands to go into his *rondaval*.

There is much discussion about the identities of the theft ring gang. The *sangoma* refuses to spill the beans. In an effort to come to closure, Luke suggests that we make a count of the stolen goods. Luke assumes the paint was in the *sangoma*'s possession, so he is responsible for it. We carefully count the unused bricks and ask the *sangoma* to return them to the job site. Luke calculates a bill for the used materials. To compensate, the *sangoma* will work without pay. Everyone smiles and shakes hands in agreement. "Thank you," the *sangoma* says, and we disperse.

From the time we drove to Miss D's *muzi* to the final handshake almost four hours have passed. Luke retrieves eighty-eight unused bricks and two wheelbarrows. The *sangoma* used a combination of 500 bricks and blocks, eight thatch poles, and twenty liters of paint. The bill for the *sangoma* is more than 4,000 rand. The economic end result: Luke gets back about 1,000 rand worth of materials and a worker for ten days valued at about 300 rand. He has a quantifiable loss of more than 3,000 rand, probably much more. Luke and his foreman spent four hours of their workday dealing with the situation. The social end result: the *sangoma* is caught and reprimanded, there is no ugly scene, no threat of violence, and no retribution.

When I drop Miss D off at her *muzi*, I ask what the *sangoma's gogo* yelled as she ran past us. Miss D replies with a grin, "She said 'I told you you would get into trouble if you took stolen goods!'" The following day I walk past the *sangoma* on my way to the lodge. He greets me warmly with how-do-you-dos and thank-yous like we are good friends and I have done him a favor. Western values meet African social order, where harmony takes precedence over economic parity.

If the *sangoma* had had the foresight to hold off using the red bricks and thatch poles for two weeks, Luke would have been gone. The *sangoma* could have kept the pilfered items and could possibly have benefited from more stolen goods. His impatient behavior doesn't speak well for his ability as a diviner! Some might say the *sangoma* needed more patience. I think he needed some good old-fashioned common sense.

The epilogue to the story is that the houses are completed to the approval of all involved. Miss D tells me that after Luke and his crew left the area the *sangoma* spread the rumor that Luke ran away without paying him for his last three weeks' labor. The *sangoma* boasted that if Luke ever returned he would "take care of him." Saving face, Zulu style.

While moving into my new residence, I notice a beautiful design at the driveway entrance made from whitewashed rocks. Miss D tells me the *sangoma* made it. I ask if the design is a blessing or a curse. She smiles and shrugs.

Chapter 16:
Doing Business in South Africa

A SIGNIFICANT FOCUS OF WILD'S LEADERSHIP TRAINING is to develop professional and ethical business attitudes and practices. Being victimized by men and authority figures looms large in the female Zulu psyche, creating an attitude of apathy. I consciously make an effort to change that pattern by both example and verbal encouragement. When I have a problem dealing with a business, such as putting Miss D onto our insurance policy as a driver for the *bakkie* or getting her listed on our bank account, I always include her in the process. For better or worse, my tactics seem to be working. Miss D is more assertive, more vocal, and more willing to stand up to men and the tribal council when she feels a wrong has been committed. Toward the end of my stay, she shows me how far she has come.

The WILD Foundation wants to help a school dance troop. The troop does not own traditional costumes, which prevents them from performing at the lodge and other venues. WILD provides as part loan, part grant monies to pay for antelope skins gathered from animals raised on farms for food. The dance troop will use the skins to make costumes and then repay the loan from proceeds of their performances.

I ask Miss D if she knows where we can get the skins. Mr. Mazibuko in Newcastle has a source. She negotiates the price with Mr. Mazibuko, determines the number of skins required, and places the order. Mr. Mazibuko submits an invoice for the full amount and insists that the amount be paid in full before he can deliver the skins. I warn Miss D that that is not a very good business practice, but she insists he can be trusted. I want her to assume more responsibility, so I tell her it's her choice. She pays the invoice in full.

Months go by and no skins are delivered. I let Miss D handle the situation. She makes several phone calls. More time passes—still no skins. I ask her to inform Mr. Mazibuko that The WILD Foundation will take legal action if we do not get the skins. She says she will take care of it. Using the *bakkie*, she drives to Newcastle to find Mr. Mazibuko. His family gives her the runaround—sending her from one end of town to the other trying to find the illusive gentleman. She makes an appointment to return in a few days, and again she is pointed in every direction but his. Wisely, she has brought the purchase agreement for the skins and the payment records with her. She locates the police station and tells a policeman what has transpired.

The policeman says he knows Mr. Mazibuko and accompanies Miss D on a mission to find him. Mr. Mazibuko has been hiding out in an associate's house. He informs Miss D that the supplier of the skins has failed him. He will send the skins as soon as he gets them. Miss D demands that the money be refunded. In the presence of the policeman, Mr. Mazibuko promises to deposit the funds he owes us into our account within two days. A week goes by and only half the money owed has been deposited. Miss D once again drives to Newcastle and goes straight to the police station. She finds the policeman who helped her, shows him the documentation, and asks for further assistance. When they find Mr. Mazibuko, the police officer draws his gun and says that if he does not pay the balance immediately he will be put in jail. The policeman and Miss D accompany Mr. Mazibuko to the bank and stay with him while he deposits the balance. We later discover that Mr. Mazibuko's source for the skins is an illegal poacher.

Bust my buttons—I'm so proud of Miss D. She made a mistake in judgment but rose to the occasion with amazing courage, problem-solving ability, and tenacity. It has been a wonderful lesson is business management.

As for myself, I adapt as well as I can in a difficult business environment. Take for example banking fees. In South Africa they are beyond reason. Check cashing fees can be as high as $3.50 to cash *one* check. When I inquire why banking fees are so insanely high, the bank manager informs me that bank fraud is rampant. Rather than initiate systems to combat the fraud, the solution is to pass the cost onto consumers.

Purchasing needed supplies requires a well-planned strategy. Even the most commonly used items are frequently out of stock. Since I live hours from any shopping, I've learned to call ahead to make sure the store has what I need before making the trip. No matter what I ask for, the person on the phone always says they have it. At the store, it is "Sorry, Missus, we just sold out. The item will be in tomorrow." After a few wasted trips, I now ask the store employee to go get the item. They then confess they really don't have it, or they put it aside for me.

The only time I really launch into battle is when I have a phone installed at Miss D's *muzi*. Working without a phone adds layers of delays, confusion, and endless missed communications. Over the course of trying to get and keep my phone working, I collect the direct numbers of all the local and regional Telkom department heads. Consequently, I feel well prepared when I place the first phone call to Telkom to order Miss D's phone. The ensuing struggle should leave Telkom and any South African public utility commission red faced and ashamed.

In 1996, embracing the post-apartheid promises of infrastructure improvement, Miss D applied to have a phone installed. Telkom issued a service order number for her. No movement toward phone installation occurred until 1999, when a phone installation technician arrived to wire her house. The serviceman worked in her *muzi* for a few hours. When he left, he told her he would be back in a week and complete the job. It is 2001—still no phone. I ask Miss D why she didn't keep after them. With no phones in the area and town fifty miles away, it was logistically too difficult.

Here I come to save the day! This challenge gives the rescuer in me a new lease on life. Fifty, yes fifty, phone calls, four regional offices, and four months later, Miss D has her phone. Some of the reasons provided by Telkom why she did not or could not have a phone were:

Telkom: There is no phone service in that area.
Me: I am talking to you on a radio-phone a hundred meters from her house.
Telkom: There are no telephone poles in the area.
Me: I am looking at a phone pole just down the hill from her house. It is one of the poles used for my house.
Telkom: There are no numbers available.
Me: Kenny, our Telkom installation and repairman, told me

there are lots of available numbers. Telkom gave her an order number in 1999.

Telkom: Do you have the order number?

Me: Yes.

I repeat the order number, but the customer service representative cannot access it; it has been archived in the system. The service rep tells me that if I do not make every effort to discover what happened to the old order number a new order will not be processed.

Many calls later, I connect with a woman who can access the old order number. She tells me that the phone wasn't installed because the phone company didn't know where Miss D lived. Miss D will have to supply accurate global positioning satellite coordinates if she wants a phone installed.

Me: I have two phones and I never gave Telkom GPS coordinates.

Telkom: I am sorry, but we have to have the coordinates.

Me: That is absurd. I didn't need them.

Telkom: I am sorry but we must have the coordinates.

Me: Your installation man, Kenny, took a GPS reading on my house. Look up my account and use those coordinates.

Telkom: I can't do that. The phone won't be at your house.

Me: Her house is within site of this house and the repairman knows where she lives.

Telkom: I must insist that she supply GPS coordinates.

Me: Can you see in Miss Dlamini's file that Telkom wired her house for a phone in 1999?

Telkom: Yes, we have a record of installing wire in her house.

Me: If Telkom installed wire in her house how could the

order have been cancelled because they didn't know where her house was? Does that make *sense*?

Telkom: Do not get upset with me. I am telling you what it says here. The order was cancelled because they did not know where she lived.

Me: Do you hear what you are saying? You are saying that the order was cancelled after Telkom came to her house because they didn't know where her house was?

Telkom: Yes, that is true.

I look up the regional supervisor's number. Time to lock and load—I am going to accuse them of racial prejudice. In South Africa, it is common to fling the word racist around. That way, you make it a problem about race—a clean-cut way to place blame—rather than about complex issues such as competency, availability, or economic feasibility. But in this case, I think the accusation is justified. As distasteful as the situation is, I eventually triumph. Miss D's phone is installed and operational one month later.

These experiences and many, many more generated a massive shift in my attitude about capitalism and free enterprise. I left the States reviling Americans' supplication to profitability, efficiency, and productivity at the expense of basic human decency. I saw only the downside of free enterprise and capitalism: greed, callousness, and indifference. Life in South Africa illuminates the benefits of competition and creative commerce. I now thank goodness for competition and a free enterprise system. Without them, there is no choice, no efficiency, no customer service.

That said, if systems as complex as human communities can balance the conflicting needs of its members, business can and must balance profitability with social well-being.

Chapter 17:
Who's Helping Whom?

WHILE LIVING IN THE TRIBAL AREA, I have a strict personal policy—no handouts. On the surface that may sound harsh, but in the course of history handouts have only succeeded in creating resentment of the giver by the receiver. Handouts disempower by making dependent the very people I am trying to empower. Determined and strong-willed person that I am, I stick to my convictions, at least for a while.

Life in New York grew a callous over my compassion. It was easy to scorn the street people with their hands out, chic to make comments about ridding the city of the homeless by shipping them to Utah. In this place, surrounded by pervasive poverty, it is emotionally more difficult not to give. Saying no makes me feel like a selfish, entitled white colonial. On my daily walks, without fail I am asked for a job, or my hat, my shoes, my watch, sweets, money, and more. The constant requests are so emotionally draining that I occasionally spend several days holed up in my house to avoid the begging. I know that in comparison I have everything and they have nothing. I know that in comparison my life is a fantasy of abundance, theirs a struggle for survival. I must get past my guilt, deal with what is, and have the daily courage to do the right thing.

To cope, I intellectualize the situation. I place their requests in two categories: jobs needed for self-sufficiency and "gimme" stuff. Requests for jobs—jobs that I don't have and can't instantly create—tear at my sense of adequacy. On the limited occasions that WILD has jobs to fill, such as with Amafa's soil conservation project or the house construction work, the tribal council decides who will get the jobs. WILD and I maintain impartiality, but I can't escape the feeling that *I* let them down.

I wrestle with the decision of when to give support, what is appropriate to give, and when I should pull back and allow the process to unfold over time. I recall an image from my early days of meditating. In the meditation, I tend a rose garden that I planted from seed. I want a rosebud to bloom, so I use my hand to force it open, destroying the rose in the process. The message: plant and nurture the seeds of self-sufficiency, but respect the necessity for events to unfold in their own time. I get the concept—what about the execution?

Where is the line between inappropriately forcing one's will on a situation and injecting the energy necessary to allow change to occur? I decide the defining line is where one's own ego and self-reference end and an "egoless" participation in the process begins. When first exposed to the concept of "egolessness," I ferociously rejected the idea. I want to have passion, to live life fully engaged, not exist as a human being who doesn't have the capacity to commit. I didn't understand the concept. One explanation of "egoless" is nonattachment, a Buddhist construct. I can care strongly about a situation, put effort into the outcome, believe that I am doing the right thing, but accept that it does not have to go my way. Ego-rule insists on evaluating everything by using oneself as reference: one's own opinions, judgments, and prejudices. Egoless commitment requires one to remain open to others' opinions and use whatever information and methodology best creates effective solutions. Easier said than done.

Nowhere are ego-driven activities more evident than with some people and organizations offering to "help" me with this project. Before I left for South Africa, I was offered absurd self-referenced solutions for problems, like an offer of an expensive satellite uplink or a fragile water treatment system. In South Africa, people contact me asking if they can come for a few days, maybe a week, provide a service, give a gift, and then leave. I ask myself, Is their contribution really going to be helpful?

A group that organizes trips for health care workers to developing countries wants to bring a team to this area. Most of their three-week trip is taken up with tourist activities. Toward the end of their travels, they visit a preselected community where they treat the local people for three days. On the surface, it sounds great. I send an e-mail asking the following questions:

1.) What types of patients will you treat: children, the elderly, those with infectious diseases?
2.) What will you bring with you and what will we need to supply?
3.) How many people can you treat?
4.) What follow-up is offered?

They reply that they can bring a few antibiotics but no testing equipment, they would rather see children but anybody will do, and they will see as many as they can but it will depend on how their schedule goes. Please set up a place for them to work and they will do the rest.

I don't like the loosey-goosey tone of their answers, so I e-mail again explaining that The WILD Foundation is committed to assuring that in all interactions with the tribe we will not promise more than we can deliver and that all outside input is structured for the long-term benefit of the people here. I need clear instructions for a community of 17,000 people. Please be more specific.

I receive a reply oozing annoyance at my attitude of looking a gift horse in the mouth. What is wrong with wanting to come and give children a hug and maybe a toy and provide a little health care at the same time? They haven't thought through what they are doing. They just want to feel good about themselves. What if a child needs medical follow-up and they can't get it? What if they give a wrong antibiotic, or it isn't enough and no one realizes it? What if 300 people show up and they only treat twenty? Why should they think that these children need some strange-looking foreigner hugging them? It will be frightening for the children. Poverty does not preclude loving one's children. I have seen more well-loved children in this village than I've seen in many upper-class neighborhoods in the United States. Go jump in a lake. Strong letter to follow: I don't write those words exactly, but boy do I think them. This isn't charity, it is self-indulgence. Eventually I convince all involved that this is not a good idea and they can take their charity elsewhere.

I concede that before coming to this place, I could easily have been one of them, not because I didn't care but because I didn't know better. iNkosi told me that one of his goals for the tribe was to get more children in school. I assumed he meant they needed more books, supplies, and money for school fees, but at least I thought to ask. He replied that they needed fences. Fences? Zulu boys stay out of school to guard the cattle. If they had fences for grazing camps, the boys would be free to attend school. I would have never put that together, but it was obvious once it was explained.

Well-meaning guests from the lodge add to my frustration. They bring a dozen pencils, three rulers, or a few crayons from America or Great Britain to give to the schoolchildren. The gifts create far more problems than they are worth. Three thousand students live in the tribal area, where there are five primary schools, one middle school, and one high school. Giving away a dozen pencils is like showing up at the home of twelve children with only one piece of candy. The emotional ramifications are worse than the lack of supplies. And, it costs much more to buy the supplies overseas than it costs to buy them here, but it doesn't feel as good. I try to collect the contributions and wait until I have enough to give one school a token supply. My effort is still not very helpful, but at least it's not inflammatory.

I also have to contend with offers from high school summer programs that take students to developing countries. Like the health care workers, they tour a country and then spend time contributing to a poor community by digging ditches, working in a garden, or "helping any way they can." The tribal people are very capable of digging their own ditches or gardens, if they had the tools. Real help is contributing to a fund to buy tools. But the students want to do it themselves, it is their service. Service to whom?

Their intention, if not the execution, is heartfelt. These programs, although not nearly as effective as they might be, bring awareness to the needs of the world's less-fortunate people. If thought out, the people and the programs could do much more to benefit those they claim to want to help.

++++

When I move into the area, a stream of people arrive at my door asking for jobs cleaning my house, doing laundry, cutting grass, or washing my truck. I politely say no to all requests. Choosing between the applicants could create jealousy and resentment. I don't want that. I could ask the tribal council to select a person for me, but that process is very time consuming and I would have to employ whomever they chose or risk insulting the council. I have another reason for declining domestic help. In South Africa, as in most developing countries, labor is cheap. Essentially all white families employ domestic help. I want to break that stereotype. I want to take care of myself. I want to at least try to appear a little more like a member of the community and a little less like a white outsider requiring service. The gesture is clearly a drop in the ocean, given the color of my skin and my role in the community, but I think it might help. My neighbors stare and whisper to each other as they watch me hang out wash, clean my *bakkie*, and sweep my stairs. They didn't think white people did that sort of thing. Their requests for domestic jobs slowly fade away. When I move from my first house into the newly constructed WILD Foundation house in April 2001, a new stream of people appears at my door asking for jobs. No thank you, I tell them, I do it myself.

One day, two very skinny young boys dressed in clothes flattered to be called rags wait by my driveway when I return from a shopping trip. "Job Missus, please?" they ask with pleading eyes and hands held out in supplication. They have learned how to beg. Emotionally exhausted and tired of being seen as the source of all things material, I politely answer no. The older boy, who knows a few words in English, says, "Hungry, Missus" and signals with his hands at his mouth that he wants food. From the looks of him, he can certainly use it. I haven't seen these boys before. I reconsider my answer. Managing the growing number of projects in the village requires increasing amounts of my time. I could use some help. I tell them to wait and I will show them what I want them to do.

I drop my groceries in the house and return with two plastic bags. Small pieces of construction debris dot the yard. I show them what I want collected. Each boy takes a bag and sets to work. In a half hour, they return with bags full of litter and the yard a little cleaner. I give them each three rand, some cookies, and a piece of fruit. They leave wide-eyed. The interaction feels good. It is May, winter is approaching. I go inside to fix a cup of tea.

I awake at 6:30 the next morning. I lift the window blinds to see the two boys asleep on my porch. They awaken with the noise, stand up, and shout through the window, "Job, Missus," hands out, shivering in the cold. I am horrified and heartbroken. The boys are dressed in the same rags: shorts, a T-shirt, and no shoes. It is probably fifty degrees outside. What are they doing here? I should never have given them that job yesterday. I make the boys bread, butter, and jam, hand it to them, and tell them to go home, I have no more jobs.

I continue with my morning routine. I dress, check e-mails, and prepare breakfast. I look outside, expecting to see the boys gone. They are camped in my yard. I have to make them understand. I walk outside and ask the boys to come with me. The gate guard at the lodge will be at his post and can translate. The guard speaks to the older boy. His name is Sipho. The boys are brothers and live eight miles away, just outside the Mangwe-Buthanani tribal boundary. The boys walked here because they are hungry, they have no food at home. I ask the guard to tell Sipho that I have no more jobs for them. He and his brother must go home and not come back. I will give them food and tea but then they must leave. Sipho says he understands. I give them peanut butter on crackers, a banana, a bottle filled with milky, sweet tea and send them on their way.

Later that afternoon a group of four young boys from the neighborhood arrive at my gate. My "*bakkie* need cleaning very much" they tell me. "Wash, Missus, please?" The truck is indeed dirty. I sense a cosmic lesson coming on when I tell the boys that I will pay them to wash the *bakkie*. I hand them a bucket, soap, and rags. They have access to my outside water tap.

The kids attack my truck. They scrub, wash, and rinse. I check their progress in a half hour. One boy stands on the *bakkie* hood, toes curled down into the wiper blade trench for balance, trying to reach the roof. Another boy hangs off the back bumper trying to reach the windows. It *is* clean when they finish. From the look of my driveway, they consumed enough water to drain the well. Out of guilt—or maybe compassion—I overpay each boy. They dance off into the afternoon.

The next morning at 7:00 A.M. I hear banging on my gate, "Missus, Missus, job, please." It is Saturday and the *bakkie* boys are back. They bring two additional boys with them. I have created a monster. How do I get rid of them now? I explain that I don't have any more work for them. They say my grass "need cut" and make chopping motions on their arm. Lawn mowing in this part of the world is done with machetelike tools used by the men and sickles used by the women. Zulus don't mow their own lawns, they don't have to. The cows and the goats take care of it. But they do cut grass for thatch, and they see mowed lawns at the lodge and around the visitors center. Since my yard is fenced, goats and cows can't get in, so the grass and weeds are abundant. What the heck! Boys especially need to understand work ethic; they have few if any male role models.

I tell them that if they bring their own tools, I will pay them to cut the grass. They scatter and regroup within a half hour— six boys aged six to ten are in my half-acre yard wielding cutting instruments. One boy enthusiastically swings a very dull machete within arm's reach of a boy on his knees grabbing handfuls of grass and sawing off each clump with his very dull sickle. I put my hands over my face and say a little prayer: please don't decapitate each other. I return to my work.

I check on them every hour or so. They worked like demons, meticulously cutting each blade of grass even with the next blade. This is overkill, but it beats the alternative: sloppy work or getting into trouble. Let them be. I go out at lunch and tell them to take a break, they haven't paused all morning. I give them cookies and crackers, a real treat for Zulu children. They rest for a while and go back to work. At four o'clock the oldest boy, who also speaks the most English, knocks on my door. They have to leave to bring in the cows but they will be back tomorrow. I pay the boys well, too well. They shout and prance around, gleefully waving the money. It is little money by American standards but more than they've ever had. I am a fool, I tell myself. I want to teach them a work ethic and then I overpay. Talk about giving mixed signals.

After they leave, I walk around the yard and notice little plants that the boys didn't cut. I look more closely and realize that the plants are marijuana seedlings. I am stunned. I know marijuana, known in South Africa as *dacha*, is prolific in the area and used by Zulus. What surprises me is that it is growing so abundantly in my yard and that the boys knew the plants and meticulously avoided cutting them. I wonder how the *dacha* plants ended up in my yard, then I remember that the house construction workers used *dacha*. The plants must have grown from discarded seeds. I might as well let them grow; at least they are attractive. (A few months later, a midnight raiding party harvests the crop.) I also discover two volunteer tomato plants that were hidden by the weeds. I am definitely glad to see those.

True to their word, Sunday morning at 11:00 A.M. (they must have gone to church) eight boys return carrying their tools; the two additions are older brothers. When I check progress, the two oldest boys sit in the shadow of the house watching the younger boys work. I tell the older boys that if they want to be paid they need to work. They look at me like they don't understand, but I know they do because they saunter back to work. I check again later. Four of the eight boys lounge in the shade. I don't say anything. When I check again in another half hour, five boys are seated.

During my information-gathering phase, one suggestion was to never pay by the hour. South Africans have too tentative a relationship with time and productivity. Only pay by the job, and if you really need to get the job done by a specific time, tell the workers that they get paid less if it takes longer. It was good advice and time to use it. I call the boys. I tell them that no one will be paid until the job is finished, and if I see anyone not working they must leave. Everyone must work together as a team. I feel like a plantation overseer.

At 1:00 P.M. there is a knock at my door. It is Sipho, the boy with sad eyes and skinny knees. "Job, please," he begs. He doesn't have a cutting tool and there are no extras. I can't turn him away with the other boys working. I search for something he can do: wash my windows. I gather the supplies and show him what I want done. He quietly sets to work. He has a difficult time telling when the glass is clean. He has never cleaned glass before; he has never lived with glass before. When he finishes my windows are cleaner than when he began. I pay him, give him a peanut butter sandwich and an apple, and send him on his way.

The lawn-mowing job is completed after school on Monday. When I pay the boys, although it is much more than the economic standard dictates, they are clearly disappointed. Maybe they expected twice what I paid them on the first day. My fault—I know better. Manage expectations.

For the remainder of my stay the young boys, a.k.a. my midget army, become regular helpers. I frequently invent jobs for them, but it feels right. Human nature shows its color, both with my desire to rescue and their willingness to let the quality of their work slide. The first time they washed the *bakkie* it was spotless; by the third time it is barely half clean. I check their work carefully before I pay them. I've made enough mistakes. I won't teach them that sloppy work is acceptable. When I tell Miss D about the decline in the quality of their work, she says, "Zulus don't like to work on their own. They want somebody to supervise, it is easier—no responsibility."

Sipho continues to come, sometimes with his brother, sometimes without. Something about Sipho, more than with any of the other boys, pulls at my heart. I ask Miss D about his family. She says she doesn't know them but will find out. After some inquiry, she tells me Sipho's mother is dead and he lives with his father who is a drunk and a cripple. The father was caught stealing from the neighbors once too often. The tribe's vigilante justice system took revenge and cut his Achilles tendon so he limps badly. No running, no stealing. The neighbors won't help feed the boys because they are afraid that, like the father, the boys will steal from them. My heart won't let me turn Sipho away and I can't keep fabricating work when there is none. Eventually I just give him money and tell him he must buy food with it. I am breaking my own rule, no handouts, only hand ups—but sometimes rules are made to be broken.

Khati, one of the teenage girls who first visited me, understands that my generator can recharge batteries. Some of the "wealthier" residents of the area have radios that run off truck batteries they recharge for a fee at a shop in Nqutu. One day Khati arrives with a truck battery balanced on her head. She asks if I would please recharge it. I say yes, initiating another parade of kids at my door. Soon a group of regulars arrives at all hours carrying batteries and banging on my gate until I come out and let them in. "Charge please," they request. Battery acid holes riddle my clothes. The situation is annoying, but not worth making an issue of. My firm stand—no handouts—leaked from me like the acid from these batteries.

At 7:30 one morning, I hear a knock at my door. I apparently had not locked the driveway gate. A boy about sixteen stands in the doorway dressed in the black-and-white high school uniform. "Missus, shoe polish, please," he says pointing to his feet. All that remains of his shoes are a few strips of scuffed leather barely spanning the space between the laces and the soles. His exposed socks are more hole than fabric. I ask why he wants shoe polish. He says the school has a special meeting that day and he needs to polish his shoes, but he can't afford shoe polish. Sweet Mother. I retrieve a tin of black shoe polish and a rag from under the sink. I tell him to keep the polish and to let any of the other students who need to polish their shoes use it.

Although a simple incident, its effect on me is profound. I am touched that, surrounded by poverty, the school maintains a standard of appearance for the students. On the other hand, I also know that the high school management is corrupt and steals not only from the school but from the students' fees as well.

A few days later, offensively dysfunctional behavior at the

high school flies in my face. Six high school students shout through the locked security gate at my open kitchen door, "Please Missus, help with English." I let them in. A girl hands me a stack of papers. They have essays to read and questions to answer about the essays. One essay expounds the benefits of communism and revolution. It is written by a non-native English speaker in unintelligible English. The other essays are no better. I am enraged. The teacher is using his position to spread his political agenda. The students can't make sense out of these essays; I can't make sense out of them. The students' future depends on their ability to understand English. All tests, including the national matriculation exam, are in English. It is time to talk to iNkosi and the tribal council.

Early in my stay when I interviewed local women about what they wanted from me and The WILD Foundation, an over-whelming percentage said they wanted me to teach them English. Although South Africa has eleven official languages, English is the most common and the only mandatory language in school. English is required for any skilled employment. I agreed to teach English and enthusiastically embraced my role, starting with a crusade to locate Zulu-English textbooks. After many phone calls and several trips to Durban and the University of Natal, I discovered that there were *no* books designed to teach English to Zulus, only books to teach Zulu to English speakers. Every book was organized so that the reader had to speak English to find anything. The "new" South Africa should be ashamed, requiring Zulus to learn English with no book provided for them to do so. I tried to teach English classes with the books available, but my knowledge of Zulu was very limited and attendance was spotty. It was difficult for me to teach and difficult for them to learn. After several months of poor attendance, I cancelled the classes.

iNkosi knows the local high school is rife with poor management and corruption. He wants to make changes, but as with all things in Zululand, the process takes time—lots of time. When the tribal council learns that less than 10 percent of the graduating students pass the matriculation exam, the poor teaching becomes glaringly apparent. In an effort to bolster morale, the council organizes a rally at the school. I speak to the students about the importance of learning English. I tell them that if Miss Dlamini or iNkosi had not learned English, they could not have gone to America or been able to work for The WILD Foundation. Going to America is a stated goal of nearly every person in the tribe. America is the land of the free, the land of opportunity, a place where money flows like a river. I tell them that all jobs with The WILD Foundation require English.

I announce an essay contest for all people ages seventeen to twenty-six. A committee will select two winners, one male and one female. The winners of the essay contest will receive one year's tuition and a living allowance to attend the local Technicon University in the vocational field of their choice. The essay, written in English, is to describe the best part of Zulu culture and what most needs to change in the Zulu culture. The audience cheers and applauds. Three months later, only two essays have been submitted, and both are poorly written. When I ask why the response is so low, I am told that not enough tribal members can write English well enough to attend Technicon.

The English classes need resurrection, but with a more qualified teacher. I am nearing the end of my second year and want all of the programs in place before I return to the States. I dread working through the laborious Zulu bureaucracy, so I foolishly try to bypass it. I ask Miss D to pick a teacher she thinks will do a good job and start the classes ASAP. She selects a teacher, but the word spreads that WILD is hiring. Miss D is rebuked for not involving the tribal council. My plan is thwarted. Time to surrender and follow the rules.

We need a written job description, approved by the council and distributed to all schools. We must allow four weeks for the teachers to apply. News travels slowly here. The tribal council asks to be a part of the selection process. A committee is formed to review the applications. They will meet in two weeks. At that meeting, a tribal councilmember makes the wise but tardy suggestion that we should try to find a qualified unemployed teacher to hire. Good idea, but more delays. We reissue the job opportunity flyers, specifically requesting applications from unemployed teachers. Because it is near the summer/Christmas holiday, we are asked to give applicants through the second week in January to apply—that is six weeks away. So be it.

By the third week in January, *no* applications from unemployed teachers have been received. Now we need to redistribute the notice for the teaching position to all schools in the area, requesting working teachers apply and allowing three weeks for them to do so. With more delays, missed appointments, and the usual communication challenges, the interviews aren't complete until the mid-April. Classes begin the first week in May. I tried to hire a teacher in September—the official process is completed in May. And people ask how come everything takes so long?

Within weeks, the classes are full. One student improves his English enough to get a job in town. It is too early to tell if these classes will improve matriculation rates, but if their only achievement is that one young man gets a job, they are a success.

Chapter 18: Problem Solving

ZULUS ARE WARRIORS. From the days of King Shaka, the great Zulu warrior chief, through apartheid, Zulus cultivated a violent warlike society where men gained self-worth as fearless fighters. They earned the justifiable reputation as one of the fiercest enemies that the British, or anyone else, could face in battle. With no more wars or enemies to conquer, their need to express aggression turned inward. Clan warfare became common and vicious. Combined with the psychological toll of apartheid, where proud and worthy men were treated as stupid, immoral boys, their culture today accepts violence as inevitable. Under apartheid, blacks were excluded from participating in government, business, and other decision-making processes. Modern-day problem solving is a skill they have yet to embrace. Problem solving Zulu style involves talking a problem to death, ignoring the problem, or killing the source of the problem. It may be effective in the short term, but it is highly ineffective in the long term.

Family feuds, the roots of which are buried deep within the

soil of Zulu history, continue to this day. Somebody killed somebody, there was retaliation, and on and on—such as the *gogo* who,
seventy-five years later, will still not eat chicken. I vividly remember, a little too vividly, lying in bed listening to gunfire, counting
the shots as the shooting moves closer. Should I get on the floor?
I don't need a stray bullet entering through the window and hitting me while I lie in bed. Before I mobilize to take cover, the
shooting stops. The next morning I ask Miss D about the gun-
play. A family feud dating back to the early 1960s flared up.
Feuding family members, tanked up on beer, decided to have
another go at each other.

The lack of problem-solving skills is disturbingly evident in a
situation involving three young boys. Our house contractor hires
the boys, at the boys' request, to line the center strip of the driveway with small rocks. When they demand pay at the end of their
first workday, Luke tells them they will be paid at the end of next
week along with all the other workers. The boys are not happy,
they want their money now. For safety reasons, Luke never keeps
cash at the building site; he brings it in for paydays only.

The next day Luke is gone, but his assistant is on-site. Again,
the boys ask for their pay. The assistant tells them that they will
be paid on payday. The boys, not pleased with that answer, decide
to take matters into their own hands. After dark, they sneak onto
the building site and spend the night removing all of the stones
they had put in place, damaging the fence in the process. The
boys boast of their handiwork to members of the construction
crew. The site managers are understandably furious.

Not wanting the situation to escalate, I enlist iNkosi's help.
He sends for the children who explain defiantly, "That's what
happens to people who mess with us!" I tell the boys that if they
had a problem with their employers, they should have come to

me or to the councilman for the area or the tribal secretary, all of whom could have helped. Destroying their work and damaging the fence is not the answer. I tell them that I would have paid them if they had asked. But now, since they have not completed the job they were hired to do, I won't pay them until they put the rocks back. They will also have to help fix the fence they damaged, without pay for that work. The boys look suspiciously at me, wondering if they can trust me. But with iNkosi there to witness my promise, the boys set to work to redo their undone labor. They work all day and into the night to finish the job. At ten years old, the only way they know how to problem solve is through violence.

I sent e-mails to friends bemoaning the lack of problem-solving skills in Zululand. One friend replied that the incident of the *sangoma* stealing construction materials and its nonviolent resolution is an example of problem solving done right. I don't agree. There was no violence linked to that incident, but I would not consider the outcome a problem well solved. The contractor was out a large amount of construction materials, the cost of which was only slightly offset by free labor by the *sangoma*. The *sangoma*, other than having to work for a few days without pay, gained the benefit of many times that amount in material goods and additional financial gain from the sale of the stolen items. The members of the theft ring were never pursued, and the *sangoma* was never pressured to disclose their names. I am not suggesting that the only way a problem should be solved is through economic parity, especially in a situation with a great level of economic disparity, but some sense of balance has to occur or the problems continue.

After the *sangoma* caper, I travel to Port Elizabeth to attend meetings for the upcoming 7th World Wilderness Congress. I am assisting Vance with program development. Participating in the congress is a godsend. It provides contact with a variety of interesting people, gives me a break from the intense isolation in the village, and exposes me to the issues surrounding wildlands preservation. When I return to Isandlwana, Luke's camper is gone and the site cleared, but iNkosi's house remains unfinished. I ask at the lodge if they know what happened to Luke. The manager says Luke went to the hospital to have his foot sewn up. He sliced it on broken glass on the ground around his camper. Steve broke camp saying Luke would not return. This is the tale as it was told to me.

Luke's camper is equipped with a large battery, a highly desirable item for theft. In the middle of the night, Luke, asleep in his camper, awakens to noises outside and gets up to investigate. He steps out of the camper onto broken glass implanted in the ground outside the door. He cuts his foot badly and is unable to chase the men who are stealing the battery. I am so distressed by this story that I consider getting on a plane and leaving—permanently. The incident hits way too close to home. Luke's camper is on my property. I have never lived around personally targeted violence, and in the face of it, my tolerance is nil.

I inquire further to try to understand why this occurred. Luke may not have handled his laborers and their problems as effectively as he could have, and perhaps he had a history with his men from the apartheid era, but he is a not a bad man. I watched him interact with his employees for months and his behavior was very acceptable—good, in fact, by South African standards. Some say the theft of the battery was just a ruse to get Luke to come out and cut his feet; some say the broken glass was left on the ground by Luke and his friends after a night of drinking. I don't pursue the validity of the divergent stories. There is little to be gained by it. Luke does not press charges. His men complete the project. Luke never returns.

I launch a very unrewarding crusade to locate conflict resolution training for schoolchildren in South Africa. This generation must break the cycle of violence or they will never be able to interact effectively. A woman who teaches in an urban primary school tells me that there is talk of putting conflict resolution training in the curriculum but there is nothing yet. I ask if she knows of any people or organizations that teach conflict resolution or problem solving. No. I call several Department of Education offices. Nothing. I conduct a search through the non-profit listings. The only problem-solving services are conflict resolution for businesses or local governments once a serious conflict has arisen. There is nothing on conflict resolution training. I do an Internet search. I speak to crisis intervention agencies about problem-solving training for children. One insightful representative tells me, "Children aren't the problem—it's the adults." Ever heard that an ounce of prevention is worth a pound of cure? It's time to move on—I'll put this on my eventually-needs-to-get-done list.

A pressing item on the needs-to-get-done-now list is solving the problem of establishing iNkosi in his new home. Even with his house complete, family matters delay him from moving full-time into the area. He lives with his ailing mother and she refuses to move back to Isandlwana, the place where her husband was killed. To add insult to injury, iNkosi's wife refuses to accept the role of being an iNkosi's wife. As his wife, her behavior will be closely scrutinized. She is expected to perform community service and entertain in their home. She holds a master's degree in physical education and there is no guarantee that a teaching position will be available in the area.

The royal family, wanting iNkosi well established within the community, pressures him to take a second wife, the daughter of an iNkosi, as is tradition. iNkosi's Christian beliefs prevent him from polygamy. He asks for a divorce from his first wife, but she refuses to divorce him. iNkosi has selected a new wife for himself, an educated woman from a good Christian home, but not the daughter of an iNkosi. Custom does not permit iNkosi to live alone—*amakosi* just don't do that. He needs family and others to care for him and provide a supportive role in the community. Old traditions mixed with Western morality create quite a conundrum.

Polygamy is both legal and fairly common in rural South Africa. The measure of a man's wealth and prestige is based in part on the number of cows he owns and in part on the number of wives he has. Cows and wives—says something about the cultural role of women. The transfer of title in royal families is predicated on polygamy. I assumed that royal lineage the world over uses primogeniture as the basis for succession. If there is one thing I have learned and learned well, it is that in cross-cultural interactions one should not assume anything. In Zulu tradition, the first son of the third wife succeeds the throne.

A man selects his first wife based on beauty and the promise of sexual pleasure, not for her intelligence or pleasing personality. The man, although somewhat more mature by the time he selects his second wife, is still driven by his desire for pleasure rather than by more mature selection criteria. Presuming that the man's sexual needs have been met by the time he selects his third wife, logic suggests that he seek an intelligent, stable woman who offers good conversation and companionship. It is those qualities the royal family wants in its heir, thus it is the third wife's son who succeeds. The fourth and subsequent wives are usually much younger than the man and chosen for their ability to nurse him in his aging years.

Given the entrenched cultural biases, I doubt I can assist in resolving iNkosi's domestic predicament. After consulting several authorities on Zulu tradition and divorce Zulu style, Vance decides that my best course of action is to keep pressure on iNkosi to resolve the matter while offering support and legal aid. As of this writing, iNkosi lives most of the time in the new house, his mother remains in her home away from the tribal area, and he is still not divorced or remarried—this despite endless legal squabbles and bills. Perhaps he will just outlast their opposition.

Chapter 19:
When Elephants Fly

IN PART AS A THANK-YOU for my efforts in planning for the 7th
World Wilderness Conference, and in part to help me hang in
through the challenging conditions I face in Zululand, Vance
offers an opportunity for me to observe an elephant relocation
project. I am thrilled. Time for exotic adventure. WILD, in partnership with the Kissama Foundation and the Angolan government, developed a plan to rehabilitate Angola's Quicama
National Park (Kissama and Quicama are variant spellings of the
same word, one is English and one Portuguese). Part of that plan
includes relocating elephants from Botswana to Angola.

Angola is on the west coast of Africa about 1,000 miles north
of South Africa. Angolans lived with war for forty years, first to
drive out the Portuguese and then in ongoing civil strife. As in
most African nations in the early 1960s, communist forces assisted
local rebels in their fight against the European colonizers. In
Angola, the Cuban military rallied to arms. As armies are wont
to do, they used indigenous animals for food, financial gain (selling

ivory and skins), and target practice. The end result of their occupation is a 2.5 million-acre wild area devoid of animals where tens of thousands had once lived. As part of a plan to regain some sense of normalcy for a people who have only known war, the Angolan government supports an animal restocking program. A 25,000-acre park area free of land mines has been fenced in preparation for the animals' arrival.

The most visible and strategically challenging aspect of the project is the reintroduction of elephants. The elephants to be relocated overpopulate the Tuli area of Botswana near the border of South Africa. Tuli game rangers faced culling elephants rather than letting them starve. Relocation seems like a reasonable solution: move elephants from where there are too many to where there are none. The reality of the undertaking is closer to relocating a small nation than to moving a few animals.

We need a South African game capture team licensed to work in Botswana to capture and haul elephants across the Botswana border. From there they will proceed to a South African air force base for a military airlift on a Russian Ilyushin cargo plane supplied by the Angolan government. The cargo plane will fly the elephants and the capture team to an Angolan military air base in the middle of nowhere. The elephants will then be transferred from the plane onto trucks and driven across sandy, rutted dirt roads to their new home in Quicama National Park. Wars have been lost trying to orchestrate less-complex endeavors. With years of groundwork in place, dealing in systems that make planning commissions look rational and the New York City Department of Motor Vehicles heaven on earth, the relocation is ready to begin.

It is the day before the elephant capture. The plan begins with an elaborate transport scheme to get all the people and equipment to Botswana. I fly from Durban to Johannesburg to meet Vance; the chairman of the Humane Society, Paul Irwin; Paul's adult son, Chris; a helicopter pilot; and a ground transport crew. The helicopter needed in Botswana for the game capture will fly us to the capture site while the ground transport team delivers our luggage and equipment across the border. Vance and Paul arrive on time, but Chris's plane is delayed by three hours. It is 9:30 A.M. Timing is tight, since the border between South Africa and Botswana closes at 4:00 P.M. and the border is a six-hour drive away. A new plan emerges. Vance and I will drive in the ground transport truck with the luggage and equipment, leaving enough room in the helicopter for Paul, Chris, and Chris's luggage. Vance and I crush into the tiny cab, elbows pressed against our sides with our knees poking into the backs of the front seats. Nice and comfy for a six-hour drive. It is 10:00 A.M.—time is closing in. Off we go in a pickup truck at eighty-five miles per hour towing a trailer full of equipment. I hope the helicopter pilot flies more cautiously than these guys drive.

We arrive at 3:00 P.M. with time to spare. The border crossing looks like something I've only seen in movies: rolls of razor wire, chain-link fences, and armed guards in threatening uniforms. First we cross out of South Africa and then make a second crossing into Botswana. Forms completed, questions answered, we proceed to our meeting site.

A few wrong turns later, we locate the game capture team, Dr. Wouter van Hoven from the University of Pretoria, and media folks. The plan is to capture eight elephants and have them loaded up and ready for transport back to South Africa by 5:00 P.M. Tomorrow will be a long day: thirty-six hours beginning at 4:00 A.M. for our drive to the capture site.

Elephant Rodeo or How the West Wasn't Won

There are several goals of elephant relocation:

1.) Select members of a family unit. Elephants have a tight social structure and must be transferred in family units to adapt satisfactorily to the relocation site.
2.) Drug the elephants for as short a time as possible.
3.) Crate them for as short a time as possible.
4.) Get them to their location unharmed.

These guidelines sound simple, but in practice they require an extraordinary team of dedicated professionals and an awesome amount of equipment. Six men do not just throw a lead over the head of a wild elephant and walk it onto a truck. The capture team is equipped with a helicopter staffed by a skilled pilot, a sharpshooter with a high-powered dart gun, three flatbed twenty-two-wheel semis, two of which are topped with elephant transport containers and one with the recovery container, and several trucks for personnel and small equipment transport. A truck with a crane arm and hoist moves the darted elephants, and a tilting flatbed truck fitted with a winch hauls the elephants from the dart site to the recovery container. The elephants receive the antidote to the tranquilizing dart in the recovery container; its single chamber provides ample room for them to get up and move around. The elephant transport containers are divided into four sections, allowing eight elephants on one airlift. It is a confusing amount of equipment, but eventually I see how it all fits together.

Entire elephant families must be relocated together to form a coherent herd in Quicama. Game rangers learned the hard way that elephant social structure is tightly knit. If young male elephants are removed from the influence of adult males, they come into musk (sexual maturity) before they are emotionally ready to handle the hormone surge. Similar to human teenage males, the young bulls join together in marauding gangs. At one large game park in South Africa, young bull elephants killed more than fifty rhino. From extensive observation, the elephants were unprovoked when they attacked. They appeared to do it "for fun." The capture team needs to get the family mix right.

To observe the action, some members of the ground team and I climb a rocky mound that doubles as a safe perch if the elephants decide to head our way. The landscape looks very much like the American West, with open, dry sandy ground, some scrub bushes, and bare rocks. Instead of cowboys on horses on a cattle roundup we have cowboys in helicopters on an elephant roundup. The helicopter takes off with the sharpshooter. The ground team is in radio contact with the pilot. The pilot spots the herd and dips low, forcing the herd to scatter. Elephants split off in family groups. The helicopter continues to dip and dive, cutting the selected family farther away from the rest of the herd. Once the family is isolated, the helicopter flies very low to select individual elephants. The goal is to dart three or four at a time.

In the distance we see the first elephant go down then another and another. Time to move in. We scramble off the rocks and into open transport trucks. Yahoo! Off we go, game rangers with guns loaded on the lookout. We arrive at the site. I survey this very familiar-feeling landscape that is now disturbed by enormous gray mounds lying on the ground. The rangers remain armed and ready. If a dart fails to deliver sufficient immobilizing drug, a downed elephant could get up a little out of sorts and try to kill us, or, option two, the elephant herd could return for revenge.

The capture team quickly surrounds the elephants. Two men carrying water cylinders on their backs immediately spray water on the elephants. Elephants maintain their body temperature through an elaborate system of blood flow in their ears. When they are down, they can easily overheat. One member of the capture team gently lifts an elephant's ear, sprays both sides, and lays the ear across the elephant's eye to protect it from the sun. He hoses down the rest of the animal. The veterinarians check respiration, pulse, and assess the overall condition of the animals. The elephants don't move, but I can see them breathe. Another member of the team takes body measurements and photographs. The observers move closer. I join them.

Professor van Hoven is in charge of the project. His wife and two preschool-age boys, both of whom are totally au fait with game capture, are with us. One of the boys runs to a downed beast, gently picks up its ear, and stares into its slightly open eye. "How are you?" the boy asks the immobile pachyderm while gently stroking its head. I, not to be outdone by a five-year-old, touch the elephant. As one would expect, the hide has a leathery feel, the tail hairs are more like quills than hair. The elephant looks vulnerable and helpless. I softly stroke the side of the beast, telling it that everything will be all right.

Feeling braver by the moment, I very gently pick up the elephant's trunk, wanting to get a feel for its mobility. As I bend down for a closer inspection, the elephant lets out a deep, full snort. Blasted! Elephant boogers cover my face. I look around to see if anybody saw. Everyone is busy doing his own thing. My hands are filthy from the dust, but I make a halfhearted attempt to discreetly wipe my face. I've lived in the bush too long to be fussy. I examine the elephant's feet and nails. I notice the forefeet are decidedly oval, the back feet totally round. One of the veterinarians tells me that this configuration gives them better traction on soft or sandy ground.

After I inspect the elephant, I watch as the hoist truck sets up next to another downed beast. The hoist arm extends over the side of the truck with a support leg pressed into the ground to keep the truck from turning over. The capture team wraps strapping attached to the hoist arm around the front and rear legs of the elephant. A heavy rubber mat connected to the tilt bed of the truck by chains is placed beside the elephant. Using the hoist arm and about six capture team members, the elephant is gently rolled over onto the mat and chained in place. Each team member guards a part of the elephant—its trunk, foot, ear—to make sure nothing is harmed as the mat with elephant attached is winched onto the tilt bed truck. The capture team remains with the elephant for the ride back to the recovery container.

Once safely inside the container, the elephant is injected with the antidote to the immobilizer drug and the container is closed. Portholes dot the top of the container and encircle the sides, so we can peer in. The groggy elephant begins to stir, moving his legs and trunk. He pushes his legs against the side of the container then tries to stand but gently falls back. The elephant tries again to stand, wobbles slightly, and lands on his butt, hind legs extended straight out on the floor in front of him, forelegs between its hind legs. The elephant is sitting up. It is a most endearing scene, like I giant baby just waking from a nap.

As the effects of the drug recede, the elephant is able to stand. He begins by inspecting the container with his trunk. He pokes it out of every side porthole and out the top, waving it above the container like a worm emerging from an apple. Fully satisfied that he is unable to get out, he lets loose with a fierce, earsplitting trumpet and butts and kicks the sides of the container. The flatbed truck starts to rock back and forth to the unholy rhythm of rage. The vet, satisfied that the elephant is okay, uses a long-armed injection gun inserted through one of the ports to administer a mild sedative. The elephant calms down. Now he has to be transferred from the recovery container to the shipping container. The four compartments in the shipping container are relatively small to prevent the elephant from moving around and hurting himself or the other elephants, not to mention starting to disco once airborne. Eight elephants boogying all at once could take a plane out of the sky.

A flatbed truck loaded with one of the shipping containers backs up to the recovery container. The doors on both are slid open. The capture team stays still and patiently waits to see if the elephant will move into the container. No luck. The elephant is poked with a staff to encourage it to move forward. Not budging. The team pulls out their secret weapon: oranges. Elephants adore oranges. They have been known to demolish allegedly elephant-proof fences to get to orange trees. There is a sign at the entrance of the Addo Elephant Park stating that visitors are not allowed to bring oranges into the park for safety reasons. One of the capture team members cuts an orange and squeezes it in front of the elephant's trunk and then throws the orange into the shipping container. Voila! The elephant saunters in to get the orange. The remaining two elephants are hoisted, rolled, winched, and crated. Time for the helicopter to get airborne for round two.

On the next round, only two elephants are taken as one of the darts fails. A vet and a game guard follow the elephant shot with the faulty dart to make sure the dart doesn't inject a delayed delivery of the drug, putting the elephant down without adequate care. The rest of the team transfers the remaining two darted elephants. The helicopter takes off to dart the final three. The herd has already learned that open ground means danger. As soon as the helicopter is airborne they literally head for the hills. The clever elephants try to outsmart the pilot. Every time the helicopter dives trying to drive the elephants out into the open, they turn and move farther upslope.

Daylight is fading. We watch in silence as the African sun sets behind a hillside. The elephants run single file along the ridgeline silhouetted by a peach and lavender sky. The helicopter tails the herd, driving them along the ridge. My rational mind takes in the scene, but the fantasy Western image is surreal. I hear a Tex Ritter song as elephants gallop through the Arizona desert, *Wild Kingdom* meets the Wild West.

Eventually the exhausted elephants return to open ground. A family of three are darted. The matriarch of the herd nudges the downed elephants, encouraging them to get up. When they don't, she trumpets, then charges toward the landed helicopter. In the blink of an eye, the helicopter takes off and drives the herd and the matriarch away from the capture scene. Game guards stand ready. The capture team must move quickly; there is little remaining light and a very angry elephant threatens.

The transfer goes smoothly. Eight elephants are crated. It is after 6:00 P.M. Each container is checked and sealed and extensive paperwork completed. The border guards agree to keep the crossing open for us so that we can drive the elephants to the South African air force base. The cargo plane is scheduled to arrive at the air base by midnight, load the containers, and be in the air by 3:00 A.M. for a touch down at 6:00 A.M. in Angola. We have dinner at the airfield and wait for news of the cargo plane. The plane hasn't taken off and won't because the flight crew is tired! What are we supposed to do with eight crated elephants? Professor van Hoven gets on the phone, and after some negotiation, the plane is due to arrive at 3:00 A.M. The capture team commissions a water truck from the air force. They hose down the elephants and give them water. Chores done, we spread out across the chairs in a meeting hall for a nap. The plane arrives at 5:00 A.M., the containers are loaded, and we climb onboard.

For those who have not had the pleasure of travel on a Russian cargo plane, let me enlighten you. *Don't do it.* The first thing I notice once I ascend the ladder is the smell: a blend of mildew, dirty mechanic, and fetid swamp, and this is before the elephants are loaded. The floors are studded sheet metal. Lots of stuff is lying loosely about: ropes, tarps, pipes, boxes, and a few flimsy plastic lawn chairs. Stacked in the front of the plane is a pile of enormous plane tires and inner tubes stretched over five-foot-diameter wooden frames, not tied down in any way.

The capture team, media, and organizers heap equipment, luggage, and supplies on the floor around the pile of tires. After loading the elephant containers, there is barely enough room to walk the length of the plane. I decide to perch rather precariously on top of luggage and equipment boxes with my back propped against the tires. Others flop down on camping gear, cases, and each other. A pilot walks in and makes a comment that is to flight safety what "Brace yourself, Bridget" is to foreplay. "We go. Sit," he commands, and returns to the cockpit. I choose to ignore the onboard hazards. If I am meant to die in a cargo plane with all of these people and elephants, then so be it.

The engines start. How can I describe the noise? Imagine wearing chainsaw earmuffs. As we accelerate down the runway, the pile of tires I am leaning against starts to slide uncomfortably in my direction. To keep from getting crushed, a few of my fellow passengers push the stack back into place and wedge their feet against the tires. I was forewarned that the flight would be cold; supplying heat must cost extra. I layer on all the clothes I have with me. Smart chickie that I am, I brought a book to read—

given the noise level, conversation is impossible. Here I sit, wrapped in layers of clothing, covered in dirt and elephant byproducts, on a smelly death trap of an airplane with eight elephants capable of taking the plane out of the sky, going to a country that is best known for its record-winning number of land mines, and I am happy as can be.

I snuggle down as the temperature in the plane decreases. I read for a while then look up to see a yellowish brown river flowing toward the heap of luggage on which I sit. The cargo containers are leaking. We are being flooded in elephant pee. There is a second river coming toward us from the other side of the plane. Vance is resting quietly with his eyes closed. I nudge him and point to the oncoming tide. He rolls his eyes, mouths thank you, and gets up to reposition the luggage out from harm's way. Needing a diversion, I watch the river's progress as it approaches and recedes with the movement of the airplane. I make small bets with myself, guessing how long it will take before the two tributaries join to create a substantial watercourse. The studs on the floor and the vibration of the plane form a shimmering effect on the surface of the urine. In a brief moment of lucidity I realize that I am entertaining myself by watching eddies of elephant excrement as they ebb and flow around me. I must be spending way too much time alone.

I return to my book. Finally we land. I put my book down and peer over the edge of the pile. The river of pee is now a glistening pool with little waves slapping at the sides of the plane. I glance at my fabric-sided running shoes. I shudder as I imagine the well-chilled feces-infused pee leaking into my shoes. I hesitate for a moment, hoping to discover any way I can avoid it. Nope. What the heck, I step into a sea of pee and stand there like nothing is wrong. We slowly sort out the luggage and descend the ladder into the early morning light.

I'm Alice, but instead of falling into Wonderland I've fallen through a mirror and landed in a war movie. Angolan soldiers, menacing-faced black men in camouflage fatigues wearing ammunition belts and pants bloused over calf-high military boots, surround the tarmac. To complete the picture they've donned the requisite communist red beret and carry assault rifles. Their presence is quite intimidating, which I am sure is the intention. Security in this country is a *big* deal. Angolan rebels still, on occasion, blow things up.

With my attention so recently focused on pee I realize that I have not and need to. Doesn't look like there are any toilets around. I see Vance walk to the side of the tarmac and duck behind a small bush. I spy a disintegrating wall that was once part of a small shed and walk toward it for cover. One of the soldiers follows me. Maybe I look like a rebel troublemaker. I abort my plan and return to the tarmac. I see other men from our group go off into the bushes and no one follows them. That darn soldier isn't concerned about me as a security risk, he wants the show. Screw him. I am not going to be miserable for the hour-plus ride into the park. If he wants to watch, let him. I glare at him and walk behind a wall. He doesn't follow.

The containers are unloaded and reloaded onto trucks for transport to the park. After organizing the caravan, we are off for the final leg of this adventure. Accompanied by Angolan dignitaries, environmentalists, and the press, we drive through the Angolan bush, magical forests of baobab trees. How tragic it is that this country, once an African paradise, is now too dangerous to visit. The trucks carrying people arrive at the release site well before the trucks carrying the elephants do. The dirt roads are soft and rutted—not an ideal surface for elephant transport. Those trucks must proceed very slowly. While we wait for the elephants to arrive, a zoology graduate student from the University of Pretoria who is responsible for monitoring the elephants' adaptation to their new home relates a story about the first elephant relocation from the previous year. Sixteen elephants were relocated in two groups of eight. One cow elephant died in transport. She fell forward on landing, falling on her trunk and cutting off her air. Since there were no scavenger animals to clean up the corpse, the park rangers used a bulldozer to dig a trench and bury her. The newly relocated elephant herd was understandably disoriented in their new surrounding, each day roaming over a greater range than is typical. Despite their wanderings, every day for two weeks the elephants returned to the site where the cow was buried. One elephant would break a branch off a tree or uproot an entire tree and drag it on top of her grave. I am deeply touched by this story of awareness, wisdom, and mourning.

When the elephants arrive, the observers vie for position, competing to secure the best view and still be out of harm's way. Some climb a low mound, some climb onto truck roofs, and some slide beneath the trucks using the tires for cover. It is a good bet that the elephants won't be happy when they are released. A scared elephant, or one feeling threatened, is likely to charge.

Each elephant has its own style for stepping out into its new home. The first elephant walks out, turns, flares her ears threatening to charge, looks around, reconsiders, and runs into the bush. The observers cheer and the Angolan generals toast each other in Russian with a Coca-Cola. The second elephant walks out of the container straight toward a tree, starts eating the leaves, looks around, realizes he is not alone, and trots off into the bush. Another elephant, noticeably indignant, walks out, picks up sand in her trunk, and throws it at us before stomping off. Another bolts out of the container, running headlong to the bush and never looking back.

The eighth and final elephant creates a challenge. During transport, she fell over on her side, or perhaps intentionally lay down, slipping her legs under the bars that divide the container. The elephant is unharmed, but because of the confined space she can't maneuver to stand up. While senior members of the capture team huddle to formulate a plan to get her out, one attendant places a pail of water near the elephant for her to drink. Lying helplessly pinned, she manages to grab the pail with her trunk and throw it at the attendant. She swings her trunk wildly at anyone who tries to come near. By now, the press and Angolan observers are getting rowdy. The capture team wants the observers to leave to create a calmer environment for the elephant and the people working to release her. The press, understandably suspicious, complain that we want them to leave so that we can "dispose" of the problem and hide our failure. After a lot of persuasion, most of the press and observers depart. A few press remain to document the saga of the eighth elephant.

The team wants to avoid darting her again. She has been through enough trauma and more drugs may harm her. They enter the container with a hacksaw to cut the bars, but the elephant will have none of that. She fights back as best she can. One vet limps away after she lands a swift but fortunately weak kick. She could easily have shattered his leg. The vets worry that she may become dehydrated or injured as she fights off her rescuers. For her own safety, the elephant is darted with an immobilizing drug. The bars of the container are cut and the elephant receives the antidote. We wait quietly. She struggles to her feet, gains her balance, and steps out of the container, mad, mad, mad. She rams a truck holding observers. If she tries, she could roll the truck and crush its occupants. We look on in fear. Fortunately, after one more halfhearted bash to the side of the truck she runs off into the bush unharmed.

All eight elephants are released alive and well. It has been thirty-six hours since we began. So much effort for seemingly so little gain, but like a series of events each so small they hardly matter, once accumulated their impact is profound. In less than twenty-four hours the team flies back to Botswana to bring the next eight elephants and then zebra, giraffe, and antelope. It is a small beginning, but isn't that how all dreams start?

Chapter 20:
7th World Wilderness Congress

Courtesy of The WILD Foundation

MY HELP WITH PROGRAM DEVELOPMENT for the 7th World Wilderness Congress is a minimal contribution compared to the pivotal role of program manager. Consequently, I feel ill prepared when, six weeks before the congress opens, Vance asks me to take over this position. The existing program manager has withdrawn— her father is dying and her fiancé is ill. I am qualified for the position but concerned that after such a slow, somewhat dull pace of Isandlwana, I will be unable to rally the energy for the eighteen-hour days required to keep the program flowing. Can I interact with hundreds of delegates and presenters and manage the complex logistics? Can I find the stamina to match the needs of the job? I can and I do.

For a variety of logistical reasons, this congress only has eleven months of preparation time, far shorter than the minimum two-plus years usually allotted for the process. Funds need to be raised, themes and presenters organized, and governmental authorities persuaded to participate. This is not a typical four-day talking heads' conference. In fact, Vance insists that no one call it a conference. He fines anyone who does one dollar. For Vance the term *congress* means a coming together of representatives as equals, to discuss and share. He feels the term *conference* means the informed preaching to the assembled. The congress spans eight days with an average of 800 attendees. It begins with an opening ceremony drawn from the culture and traditions of the host country, has a two-day plenary session with presentations on a variety of topics, a one-day break for trips to places of interest, and then divides into working sessions, focus groups, discussion groups, and poster presentations. All of this is accompanied by art, dance, music, theater, and cultural events. As part of the cultural exhibits, twenty EMBO Craft wall hangings from rural tribes all over South Africa decorate the main lecture hall. They are magnificent. Delegates fight over the art, vying for the chance to purchase them.

Andrew Muir, the head of the Wilderness Foundation, the South African sister organization to WILD, is our in-country host for the congress. He plans a gala evening in honor of Dr. Player's retirement, including a dance party on the beach hosted by the mayor of Port Elizabeth. WILD sponsors an environmental film festival open to the public. During meeting breaks, music and dance troupes perform traditional works. The internationally renowned Soweto String Quartet closes the WWC with a concert. Professional training workshops are scheduled for the weeks bracketing the congress. It is a lot to accomplish.

I ask Vance why he designs so complicated an event. Why all the cultural stuff—why not just say what you want to say and allow the participants to entertain themselves? Vance explains that wilderness is not about the singular concept of nature. It encompasses all aspects of the human condition and psyche.

Nature and wilderness inspire us to create, connect us to our souls, and mold our beliefs. We are whole and we are human because of nature. When we talk about wilderness or gather in the name of wilderness, we must honor all aspects of who we are.

After months of intense focus by Andrew and Vance, the congress is coming together beautifully. Then 9/11 happens. I am in Port Elizabeth attending WWC meetings on that tragic day. After morning meetings and lunch, I return to my bed-and-breakfast. I am brain tired, want a rest, but do not feel like a nap, so I turn on the TV. CNN is available by cable. It's 3:00 P.M. local time, 9:00 A.M. Eastern Daylight Time. I watch as the World Trade Tower collapses behind the newscaster, live.

I know it's chic to be critical of the United States—to talk about how much America is hated by the world, how out of line our country and its values are. There is no question that America has some very poorly chosen values and a lot needs to be changed. But there is also a time to be proud to be an American. This is one of those times.

As I watch the quiet dignity of the people walking reverently away from the World Trade Center in stunned silence or assisting others, tears come. There is no hysteria, looting, rioting, or fighting—just grace and grit. I hear a knock at my door; the owner of the bed-and-breakfast wants to make sure I know what has happened. He turns on the TV in the sitting room—all of the guests gather to watch. I am the only American present. Each guest, one at a time, offers condolences to me personally and to all Americans. For a month after the attack, everywhere I go, even in the most remote places, people know about the disaster. When strangers hear my American accent, they stop and say to me, "I am very sorry for what happened in your country" or "I am sorry for your loss." The term *global community* isn't just words—it's real.

They feel America's grief.

Events planned around that time are thrown into chaos. The 7th World Wilderness Congress is no different. Many of the people who registered for the congress—some key presenters, government officials, and delegates—respectfully withdraw. The fees paid by developed country delegates help support attendance by developing country delegates. The cancellations put our financing and parts of our program in jeopardy. Concerned about security, government officials in Port Elizabeth want the congress to be cancelled. A very militant Muslim organization is based in Cape Town, and local officials are afraid of an attack, especially considering that an American nonprofit is the lead organizing institution. If I had been in charge, I would have thrown my hands in the air and given up. Andrew and Vance, although exhausted, keep at it. Through extensive meetings with national and regional security forces and hotel managers and endless e-mails and phone calls to restructure the presentation roster, they hold the congress together. The dedication, tenacity, and commitment of these two remarkable men are amazing to watch.

I arrive in Port Elizabeth ten days before the congress opens. With a spiral notebook fixed in my hand, I take copious notes during every conversation—residue behavior from my years on the trading floor. Within two days, I access forgotten energy and behaviors of life on Wall Street. Each day we hit the floor running, trying to meet the needs of delegates and presenters from thirty-five countries. It feels good, but exhausting. We lose some of our support staff. One key staffer becomes ill and has to drop out. Another is ill but continues to drag herself through the days.

Security forces warn us that it is not a question of if, but rather of how many threats the congress will receive. The United States is under attack with anthrax. An anthrax team has been assembled in Port Elizabeth and is on call twenty-four hours a day. Alternate site locations are available if we have to evacuate the auditorium. An underground bunker at a nearby army base serves as a command post for national security forces. Submarines patrol off the coast. One benefit of South Africa's many years of civil strife is that South Africans know how to maintain security without any sense of intrusion. Plain-clothed security officers are everywhere and more unobtrusive than I could have imagined possible. We had not one, not even a hint of a security problem.

The opening ceremony is extraordinary. Three groups of Xhosa dancers—old men, grannies, and young men and women—each dance separate ancient rituals defining and expressing life's joys and dangers. Credo Mutwa, a highly respected Zulu *sanusi*, the highest level of *sangoma*, offers inspirational opening remarks and a blessing ritual for the congress. Excerpts from his opening remarks follow.

A Plea for Africa

When the white man came to the green shores of Africa, he found this land teaming with animals. He found literally millions of buffalo, he found millions of wildebeest, and he found millions of springboks that migrated through this country's valleys like living oceans. He came with his blunderbusses, he came with his muskets, he came with his Schneider rifles and slaughtered the entire living Africa with his bullets. He did not ask himself why this country was full of animals. He saw people who wore skins, he saw people who lived in grass houses, and he damned them for savages and demonized them as inferiors. It never occurred to the white man that the reason why Africa was alive with animals was because our religion demanded cooperation between human beings and animals. ... Our religion did not teach us that we were masters over the animal world, far from it. We were taught that we were visitors in this land and that like visitors we must treat the village that is the earth with respect. ...

Africa mothered the human race. If you asked me what is an African, I say to you that every one of you of every race carries within him or her genes of the first human woman who walked erect on this continent Africa. Deny it if you dare. We all share a common humanity; we all share a similar culture. ...

My plea, my appeal is that we should be allowed to return Africa back to her shining roots. We should be allowed to bring back to our children the love and the reverence of animals that our people were taught from childhood to practice. I wish to tell you this: that Africa should be brought back to her greatness, to her true identity, if the environment is to be saved. ... It was the duty of every person in our communities in olden days to protect animals. For this reason, every tribe was given a coat of arms or a totem. For example, if you belonged to the Dube tribe—*Dube* means "zebra"—you were bound to protect zebra with your life if necessary. Not only the zebra, you had also to protect all animals in the bush that always closely travel with the zebra, namely the wildebeest and the warthog. ...

The thing you call ecology was part and parcel of African life and religion. We need to bring back to Africa what she possessed before. Did you know that in the land of the Zulus, if you killed a vulture you were executed? Did you know that even now, in the land of the Botswana people, there are trees you are not allowed to cut down even if you are short of fuel wood? ...

I say this: hand back the animals to the children of Africa! When tourists arrive in South Africa they are only told about animals from the Eurocentric view. That zebra there is called

Burchell's zebra. Who the hell was Burchell? My God! ... Don't tell visitors about Burchell's zebra; don't tell them about Felix Leo. Tell them our stories, name the real names ... the power is there. ...

Do you know that Africans believed that elephants were reincarnations of gods that were murdered in heaven by other gods? During the Second World War, there was an elephant called Issa in Tanganyika, and a group of African tribal people fought and died against a gang of poachers, protecting Issa from being murdered. Do you know what the name Issa means? It is the Islamic rendering of Jesus Christ. Our people there believed that this elephant was a reincarnation of Christ, so they fought and died in its defense.

What more can I tell you? I appeal to all of you to care about Africa. I appeal to all of you to weep for Africa, a continent that mothered you all, no matter who you are. Africa, our Mother.

His comments challenged us all to rethink our view of Africa.

The lectures begin. A palpable tension reverberates through the meeting venue. Environmental activists challenge governmental authorities. Hard-core scientists and native herbalists proffer their ideas, each faction vying to be heard. Convening diverse segments of the conservation world is a foundational principal of the WWC. How can problems be addressed, solutions designed, and programs implemented if differing points of view are not given consideration? If the environment is to be healed and preserved, the perpetrators, not the victims, need to change. Excluding diverse perspectives prolongs rather than attenuates the damage.

The beach party dance four nights into the congress marks a turning point. Magic happens. People really come together. Many consider environmentalists and conservation scientists nerdy, but not in this crowd. The party rocks. The chairperson of the Environmental Committee of the South African Parliament, Gwen Mhlangu, a formal and proper African woman, takes the microphone and entertains us with professional-quality singing. Uniformed park patrol guards dance with hippies from America's Northwest. Traditionally dressed *sangomas* donning goat bladders and jangles made of beer bottle tops dance with European botanists. Businessmen boogie with benefactors. We dance traditional African circle dancing, dances popular from our high school days, and anything else we can dream up. As we dance and laugh and share stories, we merge with the natural setting. The beach supports us, the ocean energizes us, and the sky receives our message. We and nature are one, a common thread for all life—a common link to the divine—however we define it. This is not any ordinary conference. We create links to parts of ourselves and to nature that we did not know existed.

By the sixth day, the schedule flows and systems function efficiently. I can relax and enjoy the proceedings. Historically, I have been more cynical and jaded than enthusiastic and engaged. I am more likely to say yes it was nice but … , rather than make declarations of how an event positively impacted me or what a great experience it was. But this congress changes people's lives. It is as simple as that. Participants willingly share those sentiments with me. Over the final two days, people tell me how excited they are to have participated in the congress. Some say with tears of joy in their eyes that they have been transformed. A botanist says he will never again approach his work with such a limited vision; a Zulu *sangoma* says she feels the gratitude of the earth for telling her story to people so very different yet willing to listen. Many lives are altered, but the award for the most changed person at the congress goes to the congress chairman, Murphy Morobe.

Mr. Morobe, a well-respected South African, is the chairman of the South African Pàrks Department and the South African Fiscal Commission. He was a freedom fighter during apartheid, jailed for many years and abused in the process. Like many older blacks who lived and struggled through such dark times, he carries a noticeable chip on his shoulder about whites. Andrew Muir, the in-country organizer, is one of the most civil rights–minded people I know. He bends over backwards to include all peoples and facets of local life. No matter how much Andrew does, Morobe criticizes him in preparatory meetings. Early on Morobe remains detached, aloof, and clearly not enthusiastic about the congress.

At a precongress meeting, the organizing committee breaks for lunch. It was my first introduction to Mr. Morobe. We sat next to each other at the lunch table. I was not used to making small talk and worried that I might say something inappropriate. We already had one faux pas by a member of the committee. She made a comment to Mr. Morobe not intending anything inappropriate, but it was and he understandably took offense. I was quiet waiting for him to speak to me. We sat in awkward silence for a while. I struggled to think of something to say. When I spoke to him, he didn't respond or gave a one-word answer. It was a very long lunch.

After 9/11, Mr. Morobe witnesses Vance and Andrew's extraordinary commitment and problem-solving skills. He warms to his role. As chairman, he is magnificent at the podium, amusing, efficient, and unlike many chairpersons, actually listens to the presentations and makes insightful and relevant comments. He adores the story quilts made in the EMBO Craft workshops and purchases two of them. At the beach party an energetic and attractive young white women from Great Britain pulls him onto the dance floor. I watch as he breaks loose with some pretty fancy footwork. Is this the same man I met a few months ago?

On the seventh day of the congress, Mr. Morobe and I are again seated next to each other at lunch. Before I have a chance to greet him, he engages me in conversation, talking about how well the congress has turned out. We talk a little about his childhood in the townships, his time in jail, and an upcoming trip to Mexico. The conversation flows easily, and when others join us, they are included.

Transformation comes in all kinds of packages. Very good things happened at this congress. Relationships established there continue. The title of the congress may be about wilderness, but its essence is human relationships. If we get those right, wilderness issues can be resolved.

Chapter 21: Late in the Day

THE END OF THE 7ᵀᴴ WORLD WILDERNESS CONGRESS in mid-November brings with it my return to the village and its lack of diversions and like-minded people. After the excitement and interactions of the congress, the transition is painful, magnified by the fact that I have agreed to extend my stay through May 2002. I cannot leave at year-end as originally planned.

Miss D has made remarkable progress learning systems that are foreign to her. I doubt I could have moved so quickly through time and technology. Yet despite her newly acquired skills, she is not as proficient with e-mail, financial controls, and project oversight as she needs to be to fly solo. Leaving before Miss Dlamini is comfortable and accepted in her new role or before the project participants have sufficient confidence and motivation to continue without outside input is foolhardy. My efforts and the efforts and resources of the people who support me will be lost. I've heard many stories of projects that faded away after the initial thrust when turned loose before infrastructure and attitudes were sufficiently developed. After several failed attempts to push tribal members and tribal systems faster than they could adapt, I acquiesce to their pace.

I regret the additional time. I had set my emotional clock to stay two years, not more. I long for a more comfortable, easier life. I miss feeling safe and the freedom it affords. I miss my friends and familiar conversations. The isolation feels suffocating, made worse by a tragedy in my life. My sweet companion Mac succumbed to tick bite fever. He survived the illness but suffered neurological complications. In an agonizing decision, I put Mac to rest. For months after Mac's passing, members of the community ask about him. When I tell them he is dead, they respond as if they too have lost a friend, their sadness heartfelt.

Hermann Hesse stated that "loneliness is the way by which destiny endeavors to lead a man to himself." If that is the case, by the time I leave here, I should be just about nose to nose with myself. And if the loneliness doesn't work its magic, the silence certainly will. My first introduction to the power and magic of silence was in the Colorado wilderness. I felt more connected to life walking through alpine fields devoid of human sounds than walking down Park Avenue surrounded by the noise of millions of people living intense and focused lives. That appreciation of silence floated away like smoke from an extinguished fire when I returned to "civilization."

Volumes have been written on the transformative power of solitude and silence. Eastern religions espouse solitude and silence as a path to knowing the divine. Most religious initiations require a period of silent solitude. The silence here is ever present. It becomes my teacher. There is nowhere to hide from thoughts I don't want to think or feelings I don't want to feel. My beliefs, judgments, anxieties, and desires bubble to the surface of my consciousness like gas escaping from a swamp, forcing me to examine them. Anger that I refused to acknowledge demands to be recognized. In silence I learn that my anger always stems from fear of something. I get angry because I am afraid of failing, afraid of being used, or afraid of being inadequate to the task. When I confront my fear the anger dissipates. In silence I find peace.

++++

To help ease the burden of my extended stay and to see how Miss D will fare on her own, I plan a break at Christmas, returning to South Africa in mid-January. No significant problems occur in my four-week absence, but not much is accomplished either. This is in part due to the usual Zulu time line, in part the inability to get anything done over the summer holiday, and in part from the lack of anyone encouraging a move forward.

Over the next three months, we make good progress. Vance suggests that we hire four helpers for Miss D, one from each ward. The helpers can act as her eyes and ears in their respective neighborhoods, smoothing the omnipresent challenge of communication in a place without phones or cars. Additionally, the new hires create an image of an expanded, more-active program. Miss D gains an aura of authority we feel is beneficial, and the all-male governing council has a new paradigm to deal with: Zulu women with financial clout.

Even though the helpers are well known by the community, it is still necessary to formally introduce them to the four ward *indunas*. Miss D schedules appointments with each *induna*, a process that takes months. I attend one of the introductions, held under a tree near the *induna's muzi*. Social convention dictates that only men attend the ward meeting. The six of us—Miss D, the four helpers, and I—are greeted with lots of happy teasing and joking. The *induna* comments that Vance must be a very powerful man to keep and control so many women. One of the men asks if men are allowed to work for The WILD Foundation or does it just hire women? "Isn't it illegal," he asks, "a type of discrimination?" I avoid the obvious reply: "Isn't it illegal to exclude women from council meetings?" I instead answer that WILD hires applicants who show a willingness to work hard to better themselves and their community. Did any of you gentlemen apply? It was probably a politically incorrect cheap shot, but I'd had enough.

The participants in the sewing, crafting, and poultry projects overcome inertia and begin to function in their role as business owners. They move the projects forward without constant input. I am gratified by their progress, which contrasts sharply with my own stalled existence. I created what I could in Isandlwana. It's time to step back and let Miss D and her helpers establish themselves in their new roles. As I turn over increasing amounts of responsibility and decision-making power to Miss D, my job is, by necessity, to stand at the sidelines with support and advice. I have little to occupy my time.

I slide into an emotional wallow. Time passes slowly as I watch what I gave birth to grow into a life of its own. I know my work here has had a positive impact on the lives of these people, but that doesn't diminish my desire to move on. I will continue to supervise Miss D from the States and work for WILD, but surviving until then is the challenge. I revert to old behaviors. I watch lots of TV, and it is really bad TV, old reruns of *Eight Is Enough* and *Quincy M.E.* But I shouldn't damn the TV. A TV program brings into focus a life-altering perspective.

One evening, lonely and frustrated, I channel surf. I pause to watch part of a documentary about training men to become Navy Seals. The program filmed Seal trainees following the commands of a drill instructor. The instructor repeats the same command to his trainees over and over and then changes a small but important aspect of the instruction. The trainees do not hear his altered command but continue with the previous set of instructions. After the exercise, the instructor explains that repetition creates an expectation, which creates assumptions. Assumptions can block accurate perception of a situation, with potentially lethal consequences, especially for Navy Seals.

The show has a huge impact on me. It pulls bits of insight and observation into a cohesive message: the tremendous impact expectations and assumptions play in our daily lives. Expecting is to regard as likely to happen or to anticipate the occurrence; assuming is to suppose as fact. Expecting and assuming can block our ability to understand or even recognize the truth in our lives.

A willingness to question and, if necessary, to set aside expectations and assumptions about ourselves and others frees us to be all that we can be. It frees the child, raised to believe choices are limited, to create and contribute in unique and valuable ways. It frees the adult, stuck in an ill-fitting role, to flourish by choosing other options. If the Zulu women would set aside their society's expectations and assumptions, they would be free to contribute to their well-being and the well-being of their families and community.

Assumptions and expectations, by influencing our attitudes and actions, control not only our beliefs about ourselves but in many ways also control how people respond to us. In my hospital work, I assumed being smart was the best, or perhaps only, way I could fit in. Questioning that assumption could have saved me a lot of pain and disappointment. My boss on Wall Street held tightly scripted assumptions about the role of a salesman. He viewed a salesman as a glad-handing enthusiast who offered investment ideas in flashy packaging. Some accounts, like the one in which I increased commissions tenfold, wanted information and resources to develop their own investment ideas. When I left the firm, their commissions plummeted, not because I was so great, but rather because the sales manager paired the account with a person who fit his assumptions of a good salesman, not mine. If my manager had questioned his assumptions, he could have saved the commissions.

Managing expectations, a concept I extensively employed while trading stocks, became my first rule of engagement with the tribe: underpromise and overdeliver. If I was selling a $10 stock, told my customer the stock was going to $12 and it went to $13, I was a genius and a hero. If I said the $10 stock would go to $15 and it went to $13, I was an idiot. Same stock, same end result, but their opinion of me was drastically different. If I had underpromised on WILD's offer to build iNksoi's house by saying, "WILD has just enough money to build a simple house for you" and then built the house we built, we would probably have avoided many of our conflicts. Instead, I let his expectations and assumptions drive the agenda.

In cross-cultural work, or for that matter work with any group that has had significantly different life experiences, expectations and assumptions hinder effective communication and mutual understanding. Unaware of my own assumptions, I expected the people of Isandlwana to respond to situations using basic tenants of human interaction as defined by my experience. But their life experiences weren't anything like mine. I expected (and wanted) them to have boundaries around how much they asked for. I expected they would have a sense of self-sufficiency like me and say, "You have already done more than enough for me, thank you." Well, they weren't like me, nor should they be.

They had no concept of the quantity or availability of the resources I controlled. I suspect they reasoned that there was little downside to asking, if the worst I could do was say no. Many of my customers on Wall Street held the same perspective: asking had only upside. They consistently asked for tickets to sporting events, Broadway shows, free dinners, and more. Why should I expect different behavior from people who had so much less?

I wasn't the only one making assumptions. Zulus made assumptions about me. They assumed that I was like other whites from their world and would dole out goods and resources but expect little self-motivation in return. They assumed that I would tell them what to do and be satisfied with less. They assumed that if they stepped over some behavioral line that I would quickly and sternly let them know. When they received no sharp reprimand, they assumed that their behaviors must be okay.

The most insidious aspect of expectations and assumptions is that they rule our choices, and life is about choices. Countless people rationalize behavior by saying, "I didn't have a choice." We always have choices. Even if the choice seems frightening or difficult or perhaps impossible, the choice exists. It is not the magnitude of the choices we make that proves our worth; it is the courage to make them. Expectations are a filter on the lens of perception. Questioning and openness removes the filter, revealing choices—choices that may be less frightening than we think.

Chapter 22: Going Home

WHEN I LEFT BOULDER IN 1999, I believed life post-Africa would land me in a new location. But the longer I am away from my friends, family, and beloved mountains the more I want to return. Leaving Isandlwana is uneventful. I want to avoid the image produced by a celebrated departure that WILD's presence in the community has come to an end. I also want to avoid the impression of abandoning Miss D. I assure everyone that my move is simply a new phase and that all programs will continue with my active participation. I schedule my first return trip for September 2002.

I arrive in Boulder in June. I rent a condo, buy a car, move my belongings out of storage, and set up house. Other than the normal challenges of trying to get furniture arranged in a new space and sorting what will go where, it is the easiest move I've had in many years. I own so little, relatively speaking. People ask me, "Isn't it strange coming back to the States after living in such a very different environment?" Surprisingly, it is not. I visited the

States three times during my two and a half years in South Africa. At the beginning of each visit, it took a day or two to remember that light switches worked twenty-four hours a day and that I could come and go as I pleased, but the surroundings were immediately familiar.

As I set up house, serious sticker shock knocks me back a bit. Relative to U.S. pricing, food in South Africa cost nothing. I bought ten pounds of oranges or potatoes for 70 cents, avocados for 8 cents each, and domestically made jeans that fit me beautifully for $7. Did the prices soar while I was gone or have I just not remembered correctly? A little of both.

How much to engage the material world—the world of money and what it can buy—is a recurring theme in my life. When working on Wall Street, I listened to my coworkers' stories of glamorous weekend trips to far-off places or of buying prestigious cars, pens, or watches. They talked as if owning or doing these things filled their lives with happiness. Happiness is good, so I gave it a try. I bought an expensive designer scarf but didn't have the right outfit to go with it. I bought an outfit to match the scarf and wore both to work. The initial glow from wearing my new clothes faded by late morning. That was a lot of money for a short-lived high. I experimented with a few more purchases— some jewelry, perfume, designer shoes, and handbags. None of it made me happy. I felt cheated. Maybe jet-setting was more my style. Following the cues of my coworkers, I flew a red-eye trip to San Francisco to visit a friend for the weekend. I returned stressed and exhausted. I tried a weekend in Florida. The plane was delayed due to bad weather, I missed a connection, and returned to work tired and frustrated. Not finding happiness there.

If money and the things it can buy don't make me happy, maybe the opposite will work: rejecting the material world in

favor of loftier ideals. Wrong again. In Zululand I learn, at a
visceral level, how very hard life can be without the goods and
services that money can provide. Struggling to keep my infrastructure operational and missing the comforts of modernity
made my life difficult, certainly not happier. God bless electricity,
washing machines, dryers, and dishwashers. God bless the material world that provides them.

One evening, a month after moving into my new home, I
tear through a closet looking for something that I can't find. Did
I throw it away? I need it. I need it? What do I mean I need it?
Two and a half years in Africa reflecting on what's real, what's
important, and I am annoyed because I don't have some small
thing? Just when I think I've learned a lesson, mastered a skill, or
refined a belief, life offers the opportunity to test my conviction.
So I sit on the floor and remember the Himba.

The Himba are nomadic herdsmen of Namibia, a small
country on the northwest border of South Africa. I visited a
Himba camp with members of the Cheetah Conservation Fund.
Their camp defied comprehension. By comparison, my Zulu village was New York City. The Himba didn't live off the grid, they
lived off the globe. The area was a terra-cotta wasteland seemingly
devoid of life, yet they survived with a cow and a few goats. Their
dwellings were small domes about five feet high made of mud
and dung smeared onto a loose frame of twigs. The people were
nearly naked, wearing only loincloths or goatskin miniskirts.
They smeared their bodies with red ochre mixed with rancid animal fat, in part to protect themselves from the sun, in part as a
sign of beauty. Beauty is clearly in the eye of the beholder—as is
the smell. While talking to the clan leader through an interpreter,
I noticed that one Himba carried a musket, possibly 100 years
old. For Himba, the word *old* is very much a relative term. Their

way of living hadn't changed much for a millennium.

An old, toothless granny with breasts as flat as mud flaps started to dance for the men, teasing them with flirtatious gestures and sexual innuendo. We all laughed good-heartedly. She entered her hut and emerged with a piece of leather decorated with seashells and other found items. It was her wedding cape, a prized possession in a life where everything you own must be carried on your back. We asked permission to enter her hut. Her possessions were few: a bowl, a leather water bag, a drilling stick, an animal hide, and not much more.

Their life liberated me. These people were real, not images from a travel documentary. I shook their hands, laughed with them, traded with them, and ached for the physical hardship of their lives, yet envied its simplicity. The Himba are symbolic of my desire to simplify, to remember that whatever I have, no matter how much less than my neighbor or friend, is always more than I need.

In Boulder, my inner questioning shifts from that timeless question, "Why am I here?" to a new exploration, "What makes me happy?" I know why I am here. I am here to help make the world a better place, however and wherever. But happiness, that is another question all together. I broke through the illusion that stuff will make me happy or that achieving someone else's definition of success will make me happy, but I'm still not sure what *will* make me happy. For years, I searched high and low, made changes in my life, tried one thing then another. I couldn't find happiness—because it wasn't *out there* to find. The Buddha taught that happiness is the accumulation of good, not goods. Good works, good thoughts, good relationships. The external world, the world of goods, can provide pleasure, lots if it, but pleasure is like a drug. When a thing brings pleasure it feels great, but the pleasure is fleeting. We need more, another thing, another event, to experience the feeling of pleasure again. The cycle continues—necessitating an endless pattern of acquisition. If being happy, really, truly at-a-gut-level happy, were easy, wouldn't we all be happy? We have to work at it. We have to be willing to look our fears in the face, laugh at our foibles, get that, in the words of an immortal song, "Love is all there is." Our lives can contain both the pleasure found in the manmade world and the lasting happiness that only comes from inner knowing, compassion, and a kind heart.

++++

It is surprising how easily I slip back into the life that I left two and a half years ago. I reconnect with friends, share meals, and watch movies. I walk in the foothills, fondly remembering the years I walked the trails with Mac. I am startled by how little Boulder has changed. The grocery store where I shop is the same. I recognize the cashiers. My friends' lives appear unaltered. Perhaps I slipped through a hole in time, the life I left behind waiting for me untouched. How can that be? I have changed so much that I cannot yet fathom the extent.

The desire to change continues to seduce me; without change nothing can get better. In the past, I liked to think change could hide me from pain. It did, at least for a while, and then something would happen, pulling me back into unfinished business. But back then, change was motivated by fear. When change is motivated by fear, the results of the change may be enlightening, but the process is usually unpleasant. Wonderful insights, self-forgiveness, and supportive friends have entered and blessed my life as I confronted my fears, but I could have done without the drama and pain.

More frequently now, the warm glow of trust beckons me to

change. Trust whispers that my life could be more fulfilling if I have the courage to change. Trust knows I have the resources and wisdom to rise to any occasion. If I trust myself and trust the universe, I can choose anything.

Tallying my life experiences, I see where events, no matter how shrouded in failure or pain or disappointment, had a way of pointing me in the right direction. Like getting the pebble before the brick, life provided clues and miracles as long as I could let go of my fears and preconceived notions long enough to recognize them.

Chapter 23:
Moving Forward

FROM SEPTEMBER 2002 THROUGH JANUARY 2004, I return to Isandlwana four times. On my September 2002 trip, the best I had hoped for was that with the supervision and insight of Miss D and the support of iNkosi, the programs would not backslide. I was elated to discover that not only had the programs continued, they had thrived and expanded.

The best news of all, literally a dream come true, is that the water project we struggled to finance for three years was finally fully funded. The national water program provided money to the Dundee Regional Water Council. Because the water development plan created by the civil engineering firm two years prior was available, we were the first to be approved. A recent change in legislation provided funding only for water projects with public taps, rather than for private taps at each homesite, so our original plan was modified accordingly. The revised plan called for sixty water taps to be distributed across the tribal area. Tribal residents still have to haul water, but no more than 250 meters and usually much less. In January 2000, I believed that if all WILD accomplished was to provide water for this community, my time would be well spent. It's a done deal.

From 2002 until 2004, some program participants dropped out, some joined, and progress continued. Eleven community gardens are fenced and producing crops. The agriculture extension worker who diligently tried to undermine the gardener's work was replaced with a more enlightened employee. The microlending program remains a success; every loan has been repaid. Commercial lending banks would be proud of those results. The sewers continue with concerns about what to make and who to make it with. They still want to restrict group membership. Some things change more slowly than others. Miss D finally persuaded a group of crafters to paint story-squares and make pillow covers out of them. They were sold in the lodge's gift shop. Most of the chickens purchased for consumption in the area are now locally raised, with much of the revenue recirculating in the community.

A new craft group emerged. In a very surprising turn, several men joined together to form a wood carving cooperative. Initially they told Miss D that they did not want a loan, they just wanted encouragement with regular visits from her and her helpers and perhaps some assistance distributing their products. Miss D brought in wood unavailable to local carvers. After the cooperative sold several carved items, they requested a small microloan, which has been repaid.

In August 2003, WILD hired a native South African very familiar with rural development programs for in-country project support. Miss D needed backup. Members of the tribal council tried to take advantage of her access to resources. They used threats and intimidation to try to line their own pockets. It wasn't fair for us to allow her to bear that burden. With an outsider to report to, Miss D could transfer final decision-making power and deflect their targeted assault.

Out of our experience in Isandlwana, WILD identified ten principles for rural development programs:

1.) Manage expectations, create an environment of trust, under-promise and overdeliver. Clear, careful communication is vital.
2.) Allow local people to initiate projects. Achieve their buy-in, then guide and support the participants with expertise and training.
3.) Nurture a sense of program ownership. Create a local identity, involve stakeholders in project evaluations.
4.) Build on what's there. Provide the least amount of outside input to meet project objectives. Flooding an area with materials that can be stolen or broken does not develop sustainable enterprise.
5.) Be realistic in setting project timetables. Allow participants to adopt new practices at their own pace. Set goals in terms of months and years, not days and weeks.
6.) Respect the existing line of tribal authority, but pursue gender equality. In most indigenous cultures, women hold the key to their upliftment.
7.) Select and train local project leaders. Empower from within the culture. Be sensitive but impartial to community politics.
8.) Set the earliest date possible for transition to local manage-ment. Assure participants that outside support is not dominant or permanent.
9.) Foster team building. Local program management adds pro-gram legitimacy that lasts beyond outside support. Withdraw support gradually as local managers build coalition.
10.) Reward with public recognition. Public praise provides far more motivation than simple handouts.

These simple principles may seem self-evident, but for me, defining the process was a valuable step toward executing it. Helping people is far more than providing goods and services and more than teaching the proverbial man to fish. It is empowering people to reach beyond what is comfortable and familiar and finding the courage to change within.

Back in Boulder, the erosive force of new activities and commitments slowly etches away the daily reality of life in Zululand. The wisdom gained, the beliefs altered, and the overwhelming feeling of gratitude for my life cannot be diminished. If happiness is the accumulation of good, Zululand made me happy. Will I again live in a remote place training other people? Not now. It's time to move on and apply the gifts of Zululand elsewhere.

Two years after my return to the United States, I still feel blessed to live in a place with so much safety and opportunity. If I had the power to change America, other than waving a magic wand to make it less consumptive, I would require that all college students live in a developing country for one semester. Not a trip where students travel together and view the country from a bus or dormitory window, but one where they actually live with the people. It is much harder to turn a blind eye and let people you have met starve, live without water, or be denied economic opportunity once you have shaken their hand, laughed with them, and experienced life as they know it.

The global challenges of providing sufficient water, food, health care, education, economic opportunity, and resource preservation are massive and complex. Feeling powerless to help, given the vastness of that need, is understandable but untrue. One person, one act of kindness, one act of courage can change the world. I know it.

Acknowledgments

Many thanks to family and friends: Bob Baron, Charlotte Baron, Ann Benjamin, Linda O'Bryon, Veronique Batrus, Harlan Batrus, Linda Piette, Sherry Ruth Anderson, and Wendy Hirsh who read my e-mails and encouraged me to write this book. A special thanks to Patricia Hopkins and Cyril Kormos who suffered through the first draft of the manuscript and offered helpful suggestions. To members of my book club, Ande Rice, Sacha Millstone, Ann Raabe, Lisa Zammuto, and Julie Driscoll, who graciously read the second draft and encouraged me with ideas and enthusiasm. To Lori Kolb, whose Herculean belief in my story helped me forge ahead when I doubted myself. A very special thanks to the Godi—Kersti Frigell, Elizabeth Bertani, Roberta Collier Morales—and Madhu, who pulled me out of the fire and helped me love who I am.

To iNkosi, Miss Dlamini, Beatrice, and the members of the Mangwe-Buthanani tribe who kept me safe and helped me become a better person. To Mary Pat Stubbs who is even crazier than I am. To WILD and associates who welcomed me to their family, and especially to Vance, who believed in me.

Pronunciation Guide

iNkosi in KO see
Isandlwana e sant la WA na
Kissama or Quicama kis AH ma
Mangwe-Buthanani mahn-GWAY boo-ta-NAH-nee
Mazibuko mah zee BU ko
saubona sow BO na
sikhona sĭ KO na
siyaphila see yah PEE la
Umfundisi m fun DEE see
unjani oon JA nee
yebo YEY bo